Ian Johnston

W9-CJT-584

How
Behavior
Means

How
Behavior
Means

Albert E. Scheflen, M.D.

Jason Aronson New York

Library of Congress Cataloging in Publication Data

Scheflen, Albert E
    How behavior means.

    Bibliography: p.
    1. Nonverbal communication. 2. Meaning (Psychology)
I. Title.
BF637.c45s35   1974   153
ISBN: 0-87668-188-7
Library of Congress Catalog Card Number: 74-18605

First Aronson edition 1974.
Copyright © 1973 by Gordon and Breach, Science
    Publishers, Inc.
All rights reserved
Printed in the United States of America

Dedication

To Gregory Bateson

Bateson is one of the major architects
of human communication theory
and one of the great theorists of this
century. To me he is also a great
teacher and a warm friend.

Acknowledgments

I am primarily indebted to Ray L. Birdwhistell and Gregory Bateson for the ideas described in this volume, but a great many other people from the field of communication have also contributed significantly, including Henry Brosin, Margaret Mead, William Condon, William Austin, Norman McQuown, Glen McBride, Konrad Lorenz, I. Charles Kaufman, Kenneth Pike, Harley Shands, Victor Gioscia, Joseph Schaeffer, Marvin Harris, and Adam Kendon. I am also indebted to a number of people in the psychological sciences, among whom are O. Spurgeon English, Catharine Bacon, Warren Hampe, William Phillips, Karl Pribram, Israel Zwerling, and Andrew Ferber. Dr. Adam Kendon, my wife Alice, and Mr. John Schoonbeck have helped me choose and order the specific ideas. Mrs. Barbara Catena and Mrs. Bonnie LeCount typed the manuscript.

The work was originally sponsored by the Department of Psychiatry at Temple University under the direction of Dr. O. Spurgeon English and by the Eastern Pennsylvania Psychiatric Institute of the Commonwealth of Pennsylvania, under the direction of Doctors William Phillips and Richard Schultz. Each of these men took a personal interest in the research and personally contributed ideas and encouragement. In 1966–67 the research was sponsored by the Center for Advanced Study in the Behavioral Sciences. Since 1967 the work has continued at the Bronx State Hospital, the Albert Einstein College of Medicine, and the Jewish Family Service of New York. In part, the research at these institutions has been supported by the NIMH, grant ROI-MH15977. Dr. Israel Zwerling, Director of the Bronx State Hospital, and Mr. Stanford Sherman, of the Jewish Family Service, have been particularly supportive of the work in the past two years.

Contents

How
Behavior
Means

Preface   The Background

For many decades there has been a standing argument among various disciplines about how meaning is conveyed in human communication. In recent years, new data have emerged about non-language behavior, resulting in a new, and very different, point of view.

In the presystems era, before World War II, a number of separate disciplines were concerned with various aspects of language, communication, and meaning. Among these were semiotics, semantics, general semantics, pragmatics, psychiatry and psychoanalysis, psycholinguistics, and structural linguistics.[1] But the issue of meaning was very elusive. The psychologically oriented sciences generally ended up with inferences and deductions about the motives or personality traits of separate speakers. The structural linguists described the forms of language but generally avoided the issue of meaning as insolvable. Most of us followed the lexicographers and repeated what we learned in third-grade English. Words referred to places, things, and events. So we made lists of words, and after these we jotted down other words that represented their meanings. We believed that communication occurred when the use of words evoked a memory of these meanings in a listener.

But these kiddie concepts of meaning and communication could not stand up to reality. We knew, for example, that a word often had so many possible denotations that

[1] Descriptions of these disciplines have been made by writers such as Carnap (1947), Korzybski (1948), Sapir (1921), Bloomfield (1933), Z. Harris (1951), and Cherry (1961).

its use did not convey any particular or specific meaning. We knew as well that in one situation a given word or phrase conveyed one kind of connotation while the same word a few moments later carried a very different set of innuendos. In fact, an utterance often carried implications far different from or even opposite to what was said in the words.

In the 1970s we can look back and understand why earlier workers could not come up with more comprehensive ideas about meaning. In the first place, they paid attention only to verbal forms or at most only to speech. And they looked for meaning in the forms of speech rather than in the relationship between form and context.

Why was so narrow a perspective then in vogue? Before the conceptual revolution of the 1940s and 1950s an Aristotelian mode of thinking and research prevailed in most sciences and in all the sciences of man. Some real or single truth, some essence, was sought by taking a complex phenomenon apart stone by stone, looking for the "answer" in each atomistic tidbit. So communication was reduced to the separate actions of participants; and the multichanneled process of communicational behavior was reduced to language, which in turn was reduced to words. We could not find meaning in words, any more than we could find consciousness in a nerve cell or love in a gonad. The problem of meaning had to wait for a more holistic notion of science and the new data that such a perspective could make available.

Since 1950, a systems view of human communication has gradually emerged. A first step, inadequate but challenging, developed in the mid-1950s, when information theory (Shannon and Weaver, 1949; Colby, 1960) was applied to human communication. A simplistic action-reaction, or interactional, model became popular. More sophisticated ideas of social networks and social organization also emerged (Cherry, 1962; Parsons, 1961). In a systems age, theorists were now putting things together in order to understand human communication. They described groups of people in communication.

In the 1950s, a shift in focus emerged. Instead of concentrating on *the people who communicated,* we turned attention to *the behavior of communication,* i.e., to the media of (face-to-face) communication.[2] As a consequence of this shift in focus, a picture gradually emerged of a multichanneled system of communicational behavior which the people of a tradition used in common as a code, or medium for conveying meaning. It consists not only of language but, as well, of gesticulation, facial movement, touch, interpersonal spacing, odor, and so on (Efron, 1941; Birdwhistell, 1952, 1959, 1960, and 1966; Hall, 1963; and Pike, 1954). When we knew about this traditional system of behavioral coding, we had something more tangible to deal with than abstract ideas such as information or transmission. We could also turn back to the study of particular groups or individuals and ask how each used, modified, or varied this coding in the process of communication.

The forerunner of a broad, behavioral view of human communication was explicitly hammered out in 1956 at the "think tank" in Stanford, California, by anthropologists Gregory Bateson and Ray Birdwhistell, structural linguists Norman McQuown and Charles Hockett, and psychoanalysts Frieda Fromm-Reichmann and Henry Brosin. Since then, a number of researchers have contributed information about posture, touch, gaze interaction, and other channels of communicational activity (Kendon, 1967; Condon and Ogston, 1967; Kendon, 1969; Scheflen, 1964, 1965, 1966A, 1966B, 1967, 1970, and many others). In 1955, Bateson added an idea that has proven to be of great significance (Bateson, 1955). He pointed out that much communicative behavior serves to instruct about or alter the

---

[2] At this point, a similar shift in focus was adopted in many other sciences. Goffman (1959, 1963), for example, introduced a view of behavioral patterns and rules of conduct into sociology. A structural view became more widespread in anthropology. Barker (1963) and his colleagues brought such an approach into American psychology. And Lorenz (1950, 1966), Wynne-Edwards (1962), McBride (1964), and Norris (1970) described patterns of communicational behavior in animal societies. This shift of focus in part characterized the movement from a social-science era in the mid-1950s to a behavioral-science era in the late 1950s.

ongoing communicational process. He called this kind of behavior "metacommunication."

These are the subjects we will be involved with in this book. I will try to show how the meanings of an utterance are specified, modified, or changed at larger and larger levels of context (from the larger utterance and its accompanying gestures to the flow of discourse in a particular transaction in a particular institution and culture).

Since this book focuses primarily on meaning, it is necessarily somewhat limited and traditional; it is now clear that language and non-linguistic behavior have much broader roles in human affairs than simply the exchange of meaning and information. The communicational system is a means of regulating transactions of *all* types of behavior and of maintaining social order and social control.

In fact it has now been five years since I first concerned myself primarily with those human interactions featuring speech. Instead, a group of us have been involved in the study of territorial and communicational behavior in the ghettos of New York. This research has taken us into a deep involvement with social, economic, and political issues on the urban scene. But the concerns we now share for critical issues such as racism, overpopulation, pollution, and urban decay do not preclude an interest in issues such as meaning and face-to-face communication, even though these issues have been somewhat academic in past decades. Misunderstandings, often deliberate, plague family, neighborhood, and cross-ethnic relations in the ghetto, as they do everywhere else. And miscommunication plays a role in the politics that are making us unable to respond adaptively to the crises of contemporary life. In fact, presystems theories of human communication persist, and in themselves are politically adverse. For example, the armchair notion that behavior is simply an expression of individual motives or emotions keeps alive a repressive social mechanism. It allows us to attribute social and ecological problems to the perversity of various individuals, factions, or ethnic groups. By blaming these people, we not only justify discrimination but avoid the necessity of taking any real measures to solve the problems.

To state the issue more personally, I repeatedly get mad at authors who describe "non-verbal" communication as an expression of inherited emotions or personality disorders, and thus preclude a look at the complexities of communicational processes and the contexts of our life experience. And I also get annoyed at those who tell us how to use body language for political persuasion, salesmanship, or sexual seduction. So I felt it necessary to turn back to the research I did with Birdwhistell between 1958 and 1967, when we concentrated on transactions in which language was the featured mode of communication. I dug up my research charts, my notes, and my old papers, and tried to say how we can look at meaning in a broader communicational framework.

Introduction　　The Concepts

My wife was away, so I was sitting alone in an Italian restaurant having a martini before dinner. I had just finished the communicational analysis of a series of family psychotherapy sessions, and my head was full of the data of that analysis.

Then an incident occurring at the next table made me curious: A man beckoned the headwaiter, though his own waiter was standing nearby. The headwaiter came over, looked annoyed, but waited for the man to speak. The man at the table said: "Seven and seven. Lots of ice."

I was curious about two things: I did not know what a "seven and seven" was, and there was something unusual in the way the man articulated the order. The pitch-and-stress pattern with "lots of ice" implied that the house had not given sufficient ice in the past, so his statement referred to the total situation and not merely to the drink he was ordering.

His clipped tones and gruffness were also inappropriate so far as ordering a drink was concerned. He acted as though he was angry about the past service and had to be aggressive and domineering to get a drink. But other explanations were possible: Maybe he was angry about the entire evening or about life in general. Or maybe he was showing off to his girl friend, demonstrating that he could order headwaiters around without being civil. I didn't know. All one could say is that certain features of the order related to some larger context than ordering a drink, though there was nothing in the words to this effect.

The incident reminded me of one that occurred in the films of psychotherapy sessions that I had been analyzing. Here, too, a person asked a question in which the words were appropriate to the immediate situation but the manner of saying them alluded to some broader system of events. At a certain point in the session, one of the therapists used a similarly unusual stress-and-pitch pattern. He had been interviewing the mother of the family and talking about the daughter's psychotic behavior. He had asked the mother, "Where is your husband?" The words of this question were certainly appropriate, but the pitch-and-stress pattern was incongruent in that situation. He had stressed the word "is" and used a very high pitch, the pattern that one would use if the husband were already being discussed, though in fact he had so far not been mentioned. The usual form in that case would be "Where is your *husband?*" with the primary stress on the word "husband."

I also wondered about the gesticulation pattern of the man in the restaurant. For the most part, he used typical and familiar gestures. He used the usual high sign for summoning the waiter. When he gave the order, he jutted his jaw in a typical display of dominance. And when he said, "Lots of ice," he held his right hand, palm down, about eight inches above the table top, thus indicating the height of a tall glass.

But after he finished speaking, he used a strange pattern of gesturing: He looked at the headwaiter and crinkled his eyes in a faint half smile, which seemed incongruous with his previous gruffness. Then he struck his left forearm with the side of his right hand, after which he pointed to his right temple with his right index finger and shook his head slightly from side to side.

I could make certain deductions about this flurry of amending gestures.

The striking of the forearm was an abbreviated version of the classical Italian gesture of obscenity with which one says, " 'Fongoo' a la madre." The eye crinkling indicated friendliness and joking. But pointing to the temple—a gesture that occurs in Italian and in other cultures as well—is equivalent to the order "Use your head," or "Think."

So the man next to me did not act like a customer; rather, he seemed to be instructing the headwaiter about his general performance in addition to using him to order a drink. He placed an order on his order, so to speak. This use of gesture, we will later call "*meta*communicative." It is a different use of gesticulation from merely designating the height of the glass. This use of gesture reminded me of a number of incidents in the films I had been analyzing, one of which was of particular interest.

In the eighteenth minute of each session of the psychotherapy series, someone told a dream or fantasy. In the ninth session, one of the therapists addressed the patient and said: "I just had a mind picture of you. I thought of a bowl of fruit. . . ." From the time he began to speak, he held his hands forward, palms partly upward and fingers curled, in imitation of the shape of the bowl.

Nothing unusual here at first glance. The speaker formed the typical shape of a bowl with his hands as he was about to mention a bowl. But ordinarily the speaker gestures bowl as he says the word or sentence. He does not gesture "bowl" from the beginning of his utterance. And in each session, at the nineteenth minute, someone had told a fantasy or dream, and had also used this bowl gesture even though no reference to a bowl was spoken. When telling a dream or fantasy, the rule seemed to be, one is to gesture "bowl."

I was also wondering about "seven and seven." It was obviously a drink of some kind. After the headwaiter took the order, he went to the bartender and said something to him. The bartender then made a drink, which was served to my next-table neighbor. He drank it without complaint. Later he ordered again, and each time got the same drink.

So other people knew what a seven and seven was. It was obviously a communicative sentence. It brought a particular drink, and each of those people could undoubtedly have told me what the drink was made of if I had asked them.

I tried to figure out what a "seven and seven" was by deduction. The man spoke good English, so he was not saying, "Say, Van," in broken Spanish. Besides, one would not say, "Say, Van," twice and connect the original and the replica with a conjunction. And his dialect and gestural pattern were distinctly Italian-American.

I could think of a great many referents for the term "seven." I thought of crap games, dates, magical ceremonies, and so on, but none of these referents fit the context of the events that had transpired.

Maybe "seven and seven" referred to the addition of the man's bill. This possibility was ruled out by the structure of the sentence.

In mathematical propositions, two numbers are often connected with the conjunction "and," so the same sequencing of words could appear in an arithmetical expression as appears in ordering a seven and seven. But there is a marked difference in the pattern of pitch and stress. If one is saying, "Seven and seven make fourteen," he holds his pitch and stress at the same level with each articulation of "seven"—as though to give them equal weight.

But in saying "Seven and seven" in the restaurant, one drops his pitch on the second seven and does not stress it as he does the first one.

Furthermore, the man showed clearly that the sentence ended with the second seven. His statement was not an uncompleted mathematic proposition but a complete sentence. He dropped his pitch *and he dropped his head and eyelids slightly,* as anyone does at the end of a declarative sentence.

In short, the segmentation or punctuation of the stream of speech ruled out certain possibilities of meaning. I noted as well that the junctures in speech—the terminus of one sentence and the beginning of the next—were marked by both linguistic features and kinesic ones.

Thus, three kinds of bodily movement or kinesic behavior in speaking had come to my attention. I can now describe them as follows:

1 Movements of the head, eyes, arms, and torso punc-
tuate or mark the stream of speech, address speech to
various listeners, and in general delineate the segments
and phrases of human interaction.

2 Gestures (including facial displays) supplement the
information content of speech by depicting sizes, shapes,
and relations which are being represented in words, and

3 Kinesic behaviors can qualify or give instructions
about verbal statements, in a relation Bateson calls
"metacommunicative" (Bateson, 1955).

In short, the movement of the body helps in the clarifica-
tion of meaning by supplementing certain features of the
structure of language. A word can often have a number
of meanings. In such cases, the ambiguity may be so great
that a listener cannot tell which meaning is being evoked
by the speaker's lexication. As Bateson pointed out, there
are so many possible meanings that the statement has no
(specific) meaning (Bateson, 1971). But this ambiguity is
reduced by the structure of the larger utterance as a whole.
*Some particular denotation is specified by adding adjec-
tives, further sentences, and iconic or symbolic gestures.*
And each unit of utterance is "packaged" by a system of
marking—a system of indicating the end of each syntactic
unit by specific kinds of pitch change, pauses, and bodily
movements.

But there is more to the issue of meaning than this. The
linguistic-kinesic system does not merely designate a referent such as the drink seven and seven. I summarized the
impressions I had formed from the incident:

In ordering the drink, the fellow next to me had managed to convey something about his position in that situation. He was some kind of big shot, or else was pretending
to be.

His behavior also allowed me to make some inferences
about him. He was probably an Italian-American, for he
used the typical gesticulation of that culture and he spoke

with an Italian-American dialect. And maybe he was an angry or a domineering man.

Also, he was providing some kind of kinesic messages to the headwaiter that were not represented in speech.

There is more to communication and meaning than the act of being informative. There is more to language and its kinesic infrasystem than representing some person, place, or thing by the use of words.

As I thought about this in the restaurant, I suddenly realized the theoretical problem that had been left unanswered in my analysis of the psychotherapy films. *What are the logical types of meaning that occur in any utterance?* As soon as I was able to formulate the question, I was able to utilize the behavioral data I had in my mind from the analysis of those sessions.

I could visualize at least four kinds of information which are packaged in the audible and visible behavior of any utterance.

There is a verbal reference we all know, in nouns and verbs, which is supplemented by other parts of speech and maybe by gestures. This unit is segmented by pitch and bodily movement into a customary unit of communicative behavior, such as a sentence or a larger unit of utterance. These elements of the utterance specify a denotation.

There are also behavioral features of the utterance which refer to the ongoing situation—to aspects of the conversation in which the utterance is used. These features include the tone of voice and certain other kinesic behaviors, such as where the eyes are addressed. These features also refer to the speaker's position in that transaction and situation— or to the position he imagines he has or would like to have.

There are still other features of the utterance which at first glance tell us about the origins and personality of the speaker. They tell us, for example, that the speaker is an American of Italian background who is living in New York or in Philadelphia. They also tell us that he is depressed or angry. But, in a communicational framework, this information involves more than an opportunity to assess the speaker, for we can derive from this what tradition of behavior and thought he is employing and thereby clarify some of the connotations of his utterance.

Finally, elements of behavior are added by asides or kinesic action, which qualify and instruct about the utterance. They tell us how we are to take it or what we are to do about it.

Various logical types of behavioral elements and qualities appear in any utterance. Each of these refers to some particular (kind of) context and therefore indicates some particular logical type of meaning.

A strange analogy occurred to me at that moment, which I thought might be useful in explaining this idea. I thought of my motion-picture projector. Three kinds of subsystems make up the visual portion of the mechanism. One is optical: a line-up of light source, lens, and film projects an image. Another is mechanical: it moves the film through the aperture in front of the light source. The last is electrical, supplying power to run the motor and light the bulb. Another subsystem provides audible sound.

I compared this structure with the utterance. There are elements that are audible: subsystems of lexication, of stress, of pitch, and of non-language sounds. And there is another subsystem of coded and patterned bodily movements.

My projector is blue, rectangular, and takes 16mm film, but some are more square, light gray, and take 8mm or 35mm film. A variety of styles and dimensions can be used in making a device that will project film. These features allow us to recognize that projector, that model, that brand, and that film size.

Finally, elements are added to my projector that allow me to vary its uses. I can show the film in slow motion, turn off the sound, and so on. I can use the utterance to narrate an experience I had, teach a doctrine, obtain a drink, or put down a headwaiter.

It was while I was sitting in the restaurant, then, that I decided to write this book.

Each section of this volume will seek to elucidate a logical type of meaning.

SECTION I will describe how words, gestures, and other behaviors identify a particular referent.

SECTION II will describe the structure of discourse and communication and comment on the behavioral elements that provide a frame of reference in this immediate context.

SECTION III will describe the features and qualities of speaking and movement that derive from the speaker's origins and are not necessarily a consequence of the ongoing situation.

SECTION IV will describe the metacommunicative additions to the utterance that instruct its auditors about how to take what is being said.

SECTION V will describe how the utterance itself or its gestural alternative can be used to alter or manipulate a situation.

We can distinguish these contexts for purposes of analysis, but in communication the various logical types of information are integrated. A speaker's style, for example, informs us about him in a psychological view, but it also identifies his cultural values and ideas. There is no reason, in a "systems age," to be stuck with dichotomous concepts that pit behavioral and structural views against psychological and social ones.

We can go beyond intuitive inference in determining the various kinds of meaning we experience in a transaction. The purpose of this book is to point out what is known about the logical types of elements and qualities in an utterance and identify their relations to various contexts, for this relation between behavior and context defines a system of meanings.

Two problems about the incident at the next table still intrigued me: What did "seven and seven" refer to? And what did the strange behavior toward the headwaiter mean?

I might find out by asking one of the parties. Obviously, all of them knew what a seven and seven was, and they could at least tell me about their relationship and its history. But there were two reasons not to ask them. One was obvious. The man (whose name, I learned, was Johnny) was with a girl, and didn't seem to be very sociable. Italian-Americans are known to be very reluctant about telling their business to strangers.

The other is operational. I cannot rely on subjects to tell me about kinesic behaviors, the ordering of contexts, or the structuring of communication. They do not know these things, and in fact carry classical myths about the matter that have already proven to be red herrings.

Most people, for example, are aware of only a few of their gestures (though Italians have an extraordinary consciousness about this subject), and most consider them to be expressions of instincts or other psychological phenomena. Thus informants parrot what past generations of psychologists and biologists have proclaimed. We have been in that bag for the past two generations.

In the following studies we will not obtain our data from interviewing or psychological inference. We will not reject such data, but we will not rely on them either. *Instead we will directly observe the relation of the various elements of linguistic-kinesic behaviors in the various contexts in which they regularly occur, thus observing the relation of small elements of visible and audible behavior to large units or patterns or event systems of behavior.*

By the same token, we do not base our statements concerning correlations of behavior on Aristotelian categories of affect, or diagnostic categories, or theories of psychology and neurophysiology, though we will make use of such constructs en route to our final formulations. We will define meaning in behavioral and operational terms, so meaning will be seen as a relation between an act and the context in which it regularly occurs.

I eventually figured out what a seven and seven was. For those few of you who shared my ignorance, the first "seven" referred to a brand of blended whiskey (Seagram's Seven Crown) and the second to a brand of carbonated mixer (Seven-Up). I later found out something about

Johnny's inexplicable behavior to the headwaiter. Johnny owned the restaurant. The headwaiter was new and Johnny was breaking him in.

But I could not use this incident as a source of data. The elements of behavior and the contexts are too complicated to make a careful analysis from a single viewing. If we are to study a transaction, we must record it on motion-picture film or videotape. Then we can play the event again and again to search and research each of the relationships of element and context. In this volume, I have used the incident in the restaurant to set up the problem. But, in the text of each section, I will depend largely on data from the analysis of the psychotherapy sessions, for I have worked carefully with these sequences of transactions and have gathered a great deal of contextual information.

The analysis of these sessions has already been published as a means of demonstrating the method of "context analysis" (Scheflen, 1973). But, in this volume, the data will be used to elucidate constructs about meaning.

Section One

Form: The Structure of Communicative Acts

If a person behaves in a customary and recognizable way, his action will be communicative; that is, it will evoke a common cognitive image in other people of the same culture.

Such acts are "punctuated" by lexical and kinesic behaviors (Chapter One), have linguistic and gestural "content" (Chapter Two), and have traditional meanings in a culture or tradition.

Chapter One   Speech Units

The stream of speech is marked or punctuated into customary or standard syntactic units. This is done by changes in the pattern of pitch, by pauses in vocalization, and by changes in bodily position.[1]

The Syntactic Sentence

The order "Seven and seven. Lots of ice." is a unit of speech, but it is also broken into two syntactic subunits. We acknowledge this division, in writing, by placing a space and a period between the second "seven" and the word "Lots," and by capitalizing the "L" in "Lots."

Neither of these syntactic units is a grammatic sentence. Many such units are grammatical, e.g., "I went downtown," but some consist of a phrase only, or even a single word such as "No." A syntactic sentence is not identified according to a grammatic structure; it is instead that unit of speech that is marked off by certain traditional behaviors that accompany the stream of speech. These behaviors are performed by all native speakers of a language, and one must identify them if he wishes to determine which segments form syntactic sentences.

In English the segmentation of speech is carried out by two kinds of behavioral changes:

1 A customary sequence of language sounds is spoken

[1] Many of the paragraphs and illustrations in this chapter are reprinted from a book I have written on the communicational analysis of a psychotherapy session (Scheflen, 1973). These are reprinted here with the kind permission of the editors of Indiana University Press.

in one of about six main patterns of pitch-and-stress change. One of these patterns identifies the syntactic unit as a *Gestalt*, and a particular kind of pitch change occurs at the end of each such unit. The speaker also stops vocalizing for at least an instant at the end of each syntactic unit. The structural linguists call these patterns "suprasegmental patterns" (Z. Harris, 1951; Gleason, 1955; Hockett, 1958).

2 These audible patterns of change are accompanied by visible changes of the same kind. A speaker will hold some bodily part such as his head, eyes, eyelids, or hands in one position while he articulates a syntactic sentence, then change the position of this part when he finishes that sentence.

In fact, the terminal bodily movements and the terminal pitch changes occur in the same direction. If pitch is raised, the eyelids, head, or hand will be elevated slightly. When pitch is lowered, such bodily part is lowered (Birdwhistell, 1966). Thus the marking behavior of speech is both audible and visible, and a listener can both see and hear a speaker's segmentation of sounds and thus keep oriented in the stream of speech.

In English there are three kinds of terminal markers:

1 The speaker drops his pitch level and allows a part of his body to fall at the completion of a declarative.

2 He raises pitch and a body part at the completion of a question.

3 If he is articulating a sequence of syntactic sentences, he will hold his pitch and the marking body part level until he has finished the first syntactic sentence in the sequence.

Thus a speaker not only signals the completion of his utterance, but he also provides a signal that informs a listener about the expected response. A question, for example, requests a spoken answer. We can speculate that this kind of instruction about an utterance is the simplest kind of metacommunicative signal.

The terminal marker of one syntactic utterance is often the initial behavior of the next one in the sequence. When the floor changes hands, the terminal markers of the first speaker clue the beginning of the next speaker's utterance. In linguistics these terminals are referred to as junctures. These signals are reviewed and crudely depicted in Figure 1-1.

Head movements as markers

I'm going to go downtown ..... and then I'm going over to Bill's ....

... Then I'm going home ...... What are you going to do?

Eyelids as markers

... Then I'm going home .... What are you going to do?

Hand movements as markers

... Then I'm going home ..... What are you going to do?

FIGURE 1-1.   Some postural-kinesic markers of American syntactic sentences[2]

[2] The drawings are reproduced from the author's article on posture in communication which appeared in *Psychiatry* 27:316–31 (Nov. 1964). It is reprinted by special permission of the William Alanson White Foundation, Inc. These markers were described to me by Ray L. Birdwhistell.

The subject of markers and junctures for the syntactic sentence is much more complicated than I have described here. Subunits of the syntactic sentence are also marked,[3] and there are other kinds of syntactic sentences. But this sketch will be sufficient to illustrate the idea of marking at this level of complexity; the reader who desires further elaboration can turn to the vast literature of structural linguistics (Sapir, 1921; Bloomfield, 1933; Z. Harris, 1951; Hockett, 1958).

The Point-Unit

As we have already noted, an utterance is likely to be longer than a single syntactic sentence. A speech may consist of hundreds of such units, but the next-larger segment or unit of speech behavior consists of one or a few syntactic sentences like Johnny's order of a drink. This size unit, which I will call a "point," is marked by a grosser pattern of marking behavior.

It will be helpful to begin this description with an example. Here is one that occurred at the very beginning of the psychotherapy session (Session I) to which I alluded in the Introduction.

The mother of the patient, Mrs. V., had been asked to describe her daughter's initial psychotic breakdown. She began by saying that the first thing she noticed was the girl's unwillingness to walk upstairs to bed. She quoted her daughter, Marge, as saying, "Help me upstairs."

Mrs. V. followed this syntactic sentence with another one. In a tone of mock incredulity and disparagement, she commented on her daughter's behavior: "A young girl like

---

[3] Smaller units of speech are also marked kinesically. Birdwhistell (1966) has shown that a lateral micro head sweep is made over compound words which we would hyphenate in written English. These begin exactly at the start of the first word and end with completion of the last. Presumably the head sweep indicates that the two lexical forms are to be seen as a unit.

Even units as small as a word appear to have markers. Condon and Ogston (1967), using very fast filming techniques, have shown a micro eye blink at the beginnings and ends of certain morphemes or words. Phrases are often marked by head nods.

her!" Then Mrs. V. repeated her quotation of Marge: "She again said, 'Help me upstairs.'"

Mrs. V. had been looking at psychiatrist Malone as she made these comments. As she finished her second quotation of Marge, she briefly dropped her eyes. Then she turned to Dr. Whitaker and continued her narrative. She said, "The next day I thought she'd get better by . . . ah . . . She has the doctor's prescription."

At this point Marge whispered something in her mother's ear. Mrs. V. turned from Whitaker and looked at her daughter. She asked, "Did I say anything wrong, dear?"

Mrs. V. was interrupted at this point in her narrative, because Whitaker and Marge developed an interchange. But later Mrs. V. resumed her narrative and again she addressed an utterance to Malone, then another to Whitaker, and a third to her daughter. So this pattern of speech was repeated. It is rather typical of narrative structure, even though psychotherapy is a special type of conversation and even though Mrs. V. spoke in an Italian-American dialect.[4]

The point-unit is made up of a number of syntactic sentences. Notice the types of syntactic sentences in Mrs. V.'s point utterance. In grammar we would call them declaratives and questions. These are distinguished by word order and by patterns of pitch, stress, and terminal behavior, which I will describe later.

By using declarative sentences, Mrs. V. depicted an experience in the past. She also shaped the communicative process, however, by using the question form.

The ordering of (these types of) syntactic sentences thus shapes the narrative. Such an ordering is not different in principle from the syntactic ordering of types of words within the syntactic sentence.

Certain types of words, such as nouns and verbs, represent people, places, actions, things, and events. Similarly, certain sentences represent ideas or propositions.

[4] The psychotherapy session was the first of a series that Drs. Carl Whitaker and Thomas Malone conducted with Marge, a schizophrenic girl, and her mother, Mrs. V. We filmed this series in 1959 and reported its analysis (Scheflen, 1966A).

Other parts of speech qualify or modify the picture of a referent; adjectives and adverbs are examples. Some syntactic sentences have an analogous function in the point-unit. Similarly, some words or parenthetical phrases of the sentence qualify or tell us about what is being said. Mrs. V. interjects a syntactic sentence: "A young girl like her!" which values or "metacommunicates" about the picture she is forming with the narrative.

As we will describe later, Mrs. V. also made commentaries about her narrative by making facial displays. As she said "A young girl like her!" she made a face of disgust. The daughter, Marge, also made facial displays of contempt, mockery, and so on which commented on what her mother was saying.

Note, too, that the tone of voice can be changed to make metacommunicative commentary of this kind. Mrs. V. used a "tone" of disgust as well as a particular dialect and style of speaking. But these matters will concern us later.

The Transfix

In making a statement or point, the head, and usually the eyes, are held in a given position until the utterance is completed. The face is pointed to a listener and the voice is projected for his audition. Thus, the same behavior that marks the unit's duration addresses it to a vis-à-vis; i.e., to someone else with whom one is in face-to-face relationship (see Chapter Three).

The head is not always held rigidly during the point performance. If the speaker is addressing several listeners whom he regards as a unit, he may sweep the head laterally back and forth, from one listener to the next. But the movement is regular and oscillatory and the head is held in the same horizontal plane. Or the speaker may nod at one listener and thus oscillate the head in a vertical plane. Sometimes the speaker advances his head progressively higher or farther forward with each point as he develops a theme. In any case, the regularities of head posture during a point are recognizable.[5] The transfix is illustrated in Figure 1-2.

[5] The holding of a bodily part in a fixed position during the performance of one unit provides others with an indication of the unit's

Marge kept her arm upright toward her face throughout a segment of lamenting behavior.

Whitaker would suspend his hand play with point utterances of his explanation.

FIGURE 1-2.   Supplementary transfixes of the point

Head and eye positions are not the only features of the point address. The utterance will be made in a *voice projection* appropriate to the distance between the speaker and his listeners. He will usually hold this projection until the end of the point.

---

duration, just as the shift in posture at the end of the unit is informative about the unit's completion. Thus, the bodily hold constitutes a marker, crudely analogous to a suprasegmental contour. Birdwhistell (1952) suggested that this hold, or marker, be called a "transfix."

It seems safe to assume that a rhythmical, oscillatory movement is equivalent to a stationary transfix. This principle seems to hold at all levels of behavioral integration. Thus a speaker may hold his head still to maintain an orientation, or he may sweep it back and forth rhythmically in addressing a row of vis-à-vis participants. And he may nod his head rhythmically up and down when he is listening. In each case, he defines and holds a given position and a given orientation.

In a systems view, we can claim that either stasis (immobility) or oscillation can maintain dynamic equilibrium for a phase of time. Then some change is introduced and the system of activity and relationship is stabilized in some other state for a time.

In addition to holding his eyes or head steady during the articulation of a point, a speaker will usually hold some other feature of his behavior constant. Some *qualifier of language,* some paralanguage form, will usually accompany the point utterance. Such a paralinguistic feature may be customary for addressing that kind of listener, e.g. baby talk, formal tones, contempt, or the like, and each utterance in that point may be marked with that voice quality.

If the hands are used for gesticulation in a point utterance, they are often positioned for the duration of the point. Marge sometimes placed a tactile hold on her mother while making a point. Whitaker would take his pipe out of his mouth and hold it in the air until he finished a point. Sometimes the hands are simply held in the air until a point is completed. Two instances of this are pictured in Figure 1-2.

On occasion, a speaker or a listener will hold a foot in the air or point a toe until the completion of a point-unit. Sometimes point-units are marked by cocking the head to one side during (these) utterances.

When a speaker has completed his point-unit or given up the prospect of doing so, he will shift his head position. Ordinarily he will lower the head and eyes for a moment, and he may bring down his hands or fold them on his lap. If his head has been cocked, he may bring it erect

again. He discontinues the transfix behavior that he held
during the point performance.

The Hierarchical Structure of Behavior

When we think of the stream of speech through time, we
say that it consists of a sequence of units. The point-unit,
for instance, consists of a sequence of syntactic units. Each
of these is made up of a sequence of phrases and words.
Each word is a sequence of morphemes which is composed
by a sequencing of particular phonemes (Z. Harris, 1951;
Pike, 1954).

But we can look at this arrangement without regard to
time and can conceive of a cross-sectional diagram of the
structure. In such a view, we speak of units, subunits, sub-
subunits, and so on. Thus the point-unit is a *Gestalt* that
consists of x number of syntactic units and a set of marking behaviors. The syntactic unit consists of x phrases and
lexemes and a marking system. The lexeme is made up
of x number of phonemes in given sequence. And so on.

This kind of structuring is called a hierarchical integration. Each unit of structure is said to occur at some given
level, while its subunit constituents are said to occur "at
a level below," i.e., a level of less-complicated integration.
We have above described a hierarchy analytically, i.e.,
from larger units to smaller subunits. We can also synthesize a picture of the structure by first examining the small
units and then saying how these are put together to form
larger integrations at higher levels.

Thus, particular phonemes are integrated in customary
sequential order to form a morpheme. This morpheme and
others are sequenced lawfully to form lexemes and phrases.
Several of these units are assembled by rules of syntax to
form a next level of integration: the syntactic sentence. A
number of syntactic sentences are assembled to form a
point, and so on.

At each level, the markers indicate the boundaries of
that unit. And each unit forms a recognizable and traditional *Gestalt* of sounds and movements at the level of the

lexeme or phrase that represents some particular object or event. At the level of the syntactic sentence, an idea or concept or simple proposition is represented. The point-unit depicts some particular referent, some event each could recall, together with a speaker's ideas on the matter and his instruction to the listener. This unit corresponds roughly to the necessary behaviors for making one's point in a discourse.

All behavior is structured in this way. Small units of activity are integrated into larger units according to some program and its rules of conduct (which are roughly analogous to the rules of syntax in the case of language).

This book, for example, is made up of sections and chapters. Each chapter has subsections, which contain some number of paragraphs. Each paragraph is made up of sentences. And so forth.

Non-representational behavior is also sequential or programmatic when looked at in a linear flow of time. But the units of behavior can be seen as *Gestalten,* or structural forms, when time is temporarily disregarded and each unit is seen as a single action in a time span "now." Tasks consist of a hierarchical arrangement of operations and suboperations, for example. Games are made up of halves, quarters, play sequences, plays, maneuvers, and so on. The symphony has movements, passages, measures, and notes. The play consists of acts, scenes, subscenes, interchanges, utterances, and so forth.

We can identify distinct and actual units of behavior and locate them at spots or levels in a hierarchical diagram of the larger stream of activity. We are justified in speaking of *a* behavior or *an* act, for we can define this entity objectively on the basis of its composition and marking. When these acts or units are recognizable and bring to mind a certain cognitive image, we can say they are communicative. We can also say this when their occurrence results in a particular kind of behavior, such as the bringing of a particular beverage. In these cases, we also say that a behavior is symbolic or representational.

The Position: A Larger Communicative Unit

Methodologically speaking, point-units of speech or gesture can be conceptually isolated or abstracted as heuristic units of communicative behavior. However, the head, the eyes, and the speech apparatus are not disembodied. They are not used in communication apart from the rest of the speaker's body and the remainder of his activities. All of the speaker's body is engaged somehow in communicative activities, and accordingly, the point-units of speech or gesture are but elements or subunits in some larger unit of communicative behavior.

This larger unit, I have called the "position" (Scheflen, 1964, 1966B, 1973). I define the position as a complex communicative unit involving a sequence of simultaneous units of activity, one of which may be the point utterances. Descriptively, a positional unit looks something like this:

A speaker will locate himself and orient his body to some other person or group. While he holds this basic bodily orientation, he may employ his head, eyes, and speech in a sequence of lexical point-units. He may also use his torso in a sequence of gestural points. He may use his upper body in a task performance, or he may simply orient his legs and/or his upper body to some person or subgroup, while he moves his head around from one listener to another. However, the whole body is employed in a complex set of orientation and communicative activities. When this entire unit of behavior is completed, the speaker will shift his whole bodily placement, or posture.

A characteristic positional form in narrative or description occurs when one speaker holds forth to a group. He orients his body to his audience as a whole, or he orients it to a point midway between a number of potential auditors. Then he holds this basic orientation as a transfix subtending a large unit of speech behavior. While holding this orientation, he moves his head-eye address and his hand use from person to person as he completes a number of successive point-units.

At the beginning of Session I, each person took a chair according to his status and role. Mrs. V. sat on the sofa next to her daughter, as is customary among family members who are patients at an interview. She then assembled her initial posture:

She crossed her ankles, pulled down her skirt, and tucked it under her thighs, as older women from Europe are likely to do. She sat upright, leaning slightly forward. She oriented her torso toward the camera and to an imaginary point midway between the psychiatrists. From this position she could traverse her head to address either one of them.

This is a characteristic posture for people who are going to speak—unless they are of very high status in the group. In that case they may sit back in their chair and address the others from that position.

It was no surprise, then, that Mrs. V. began the narrative. She described the day Marge became psychotic, as I have related above. Later in Session I, Whitaker sat forward and made an explanation. He used a similar speakers' position. These two positions are depicted in Figure 1-3.

After Mrs. V. had spoken the few point-units I described, she was interrupted by Marge, who made an accusation. Whitaker then began to speak to the girl, and Mrs. V. lost the floor. She turned to face her daughter and uncrossed her ankles. Thus, she took a second position. In this position she defended herself from an implication and did not continue her narrative until later.

Whitaker enacted a more complex position later in the session. Whitaker raised his head and faced a place between the two women. He said, "We're doctors of people's feelings—and we want to see if we can help ya—with some of these feelings you've been talking about."

Marge commented and Whitaker addressed her for a moment, replying, "Crazyness, you know—that's right, emotions."

Then Whitaker turned to Mrs. V. and continued his explanation: "We wanted to talk to you, and then we're going to see Marge every day—except over the weekend. . . ."

As he spoke or listened to Mrs. V., Whitaker engaged in hand activity in relation to Marge, but he kept his legs oriented toward Mrs. V. and Marge. Thus, the various

Mrs. V. explaining: Mrs. V. told about Marge's psychosis and the V. family history.

Whitaker explaining: Late in the session, Whitaker explained the purposes and intentions of the sessions. Note that he sat forward and addressed the women.

FIGURE 1-3.   Positions in "explaining"

point constituents of Whitaker's position were differentiable because they had separate orientations and distinctive types of content. While doing and saying these things, Whitaker also played with a minute object, which he held in his left hand, rolling it around with his right index finger. He directed this behavior to Marge's attention. Thus Whitaker maintained three simultaneous activities and relations as he concurrently performed three point-units: speaking to Mrs.

V., hand playing toward Marge, and orienting his body
to Malone and Mrs. V. He thus divided his position into
three modalities.[6]

Such multiple, simultaneous point performances are depicted in Figure 1-4.

Markers and the Duration of a Position

We can make the following generalization: A position
is taken and held *while* some activity is carried out—explaining, passive protesting, or listening and questioning in
the case of the initial positions of Session I. *We can also
note that ordinarily the position is held until this activity
is completed, or until it is interrupted.* In the case of an
interruption, a participant may hold the position and attempt to regain the floor. Failing this, he will terminate
the position and assume another one.

We confirm this assertion by repeated observations. If
a participant comes from our own cultural background, we
can recognize most of the activities he will carry out in
a position. They are familiar sequences which in totality
produce a customary *Gestalt*—they finish an idea or topic
or accomplish a simple task. As a consequence, we know
from experience when they are completed.

If we do not know the configuration, we have to discover it by context analysis. We have to find repeated occurrences of this type of sequence and establish that it is
a regular and customary entity.

When the included activities of the position have been
completed, the performer will leave, or else he will take
another, distinctly different orientation and posture and
perform some other task or phase. Thus a shift in posture
that involves the total bodily orientation occurs between
one position and the next. Such a shift provides a visible

[6] In non-conversational transactions, the occurrence of multiple
simultaneous activities is much more pronounced. We are now studying family behavior in the home by the use of video cameras left in
position for weeks. Family members in the sample so far rarely sit
and talk, even when friends drop in. They watch television, cook or
sew, pace, arrange furniture, make tactile contact, *and* talk *all at
the same time.*

Malone is speaking to Mrs. V. and facing her,
but his body is oriented to Whitaker, and the
two men are using the same posture and moving
synchronously.

Whitaker is speaking to Mrs. V., moving his
hands in relation to Marge, and orienting his
body to a point between Malone and Mrs. V.

FIGURE 1-4.   Multiple simultaneous point performances

indication that one position has been completed and the
next position is beginning. So the completion or abandon-
ment of an activity and a shift in posture and orientation
are coterminous. We identify one in terms of the other.
In a formal activity such as psychotherapy (especially
when the participants are strangers) the posture and orientation will be held stationary, fixed, relatively immobile,
even rigid. *It is my belief that the bodily posture used*

while stating a position is held deliberately (though not consciously) throughout the performance, in order to indicate that the statement of position has not yet been completed. It is held, I am claiming, in order to show that this action is still continuing.

When the activity of the position is completed, the participant stops, lowers the head and eyes, sometimes crosses his hands and/or legs, and often slumps for a second. Then he will shift his bodily position. The position is marked by a transfix and juncture, like any other unit of communicative behavior.

A single participant can enact a sequence of positions at a transaction and thus put together a complex integration of ideas. Mrs. V. did this in Session I. She was interrupted time and time again and rarely finished the exposition of an episode in her family history. But, each time, Malone or Whitaker invited her to continue her narrative. Over the course of the entire session, then, she portrayed a number of incidents which collectively gave a comprehensive account.

Lectures have a similar structure. The speaker may allow for questions and comments, but a sequence of ideas are eventually represented in steps or stages. Thus, in a complicated dialogue or conversation, each participant may contribute a number of positions, one after the other. *In toto,* all of his positions constitute his part or performance in that transaction. Collectively, they may represent his story or his point of view on an issue.

Chapter Two

Gestures

So far we have concentrated on the performance of speech behavior. We have said that one takes a position within which he utters a statement or a series of statements. But one can also take a position and sing, display a sign, make a face, or carry out a sequence of physical task activities or game moves. And sometimes one takes a position and gestures without speaking or simply nods, looks, and listens. And usually one gestures in a position while he speaks. It is the behavior of gesticulation that is the subject of this chapter.

In everyday use the term "gesture" is used to describe almost any kind of head, eye, face, and bodily behavior. But we will reserve the term in this book for facial and bodily behavior that is representational, like language. The gesture, then, can be symbolic, in which case it stands for a customary event or idea. The sign of crossing one's self is an example; so is the boy-scout salute. Or, the gesture can be iconic. In this case, it looks like something that it is meant to represent. The hands can be used iconically, for example, to draw a picture of some object in the air or to show that two ideas belong to separate categories; or the face can be set to represent attitudes or emotions such as disgust or anger.

The following example of a supplemental gesture will concern us again and again in this volume, for this single gesture proved to be a terminal act and a signal of instruction on many levels of integration.

Malone leaned toward Marge and said, "I had the first

mind picture (daydream) I had with you. Right then. It was a beautiful gold tray. . . ." As he said this, Malone held out both hands toward Marge, turned the palms up, and made the shape of a bowl with his hands. Thus Malone's gesture looked something like the object he was describing in speech, though he formed more of a bowl-shaped than a tray-shaped gesture.

When a speaker is describing an action or an object, he is likely to use his hands in this way—to draw a picture of it in the air in front of him. He tries to represent iconically the abstract ideas of his utterance. Birdwhistell (1963) has called gestures of this type "demonstratives." Pronouns are often ambiguous in their reference. Participants using these classes of morphemes generally point with their faces, eyes, or hands to the referents. In using "we," a head sweep is often employed to demarcate a subgroup (Birdwhistell, 1966).

In using phrases such as "up and down" or "over there," a sweep of the hand is employed to indicate some special area (Birdwhistell, 1966). Some physical feature such as an item of décor may be referred to by pointing with the head or hand.

Birdwhistell has called these behaviors, respectively, pronominal references and area markers. The term "markers" is confusing here, since I have already used it to refer to the segmental markers of language units. So I will use Birdwhistell's broader class name and call these behaviors "referencing signals."

Symbolic Gestures Replacing Speech

Technically speaking, demonstratives and referencing signals can supplement a speech morph at any level of integration from a morpheme to a point-unit. But a gesture can occur by itself as the "content" of a separable point-unit. It can have an orientation of its own, addressed to some place or object different from the orientation of the main stream of speech. In the case of our example, the gesture has its own system of marking behavior, being bracketed and oriented.

Sometimes a speaker will address a language point to one listener but gesture to another. In this case, his position embraces two simultaneous but different point-units (see Chapter Four).

The gestures that replace language are usually known consciously by those who use them. They have a general significance in a group. The group may be an entire ethnic population. Southern Italians, for instance, tend to be conscious of gestures and use a variety of them in place of speaking. Usually, however, it is institutional gestures that are consciously known and used. The sign of the cross is an example. Occupational groups or members of a social club often have a repertoire of secret gestures, handshakes, high signs, and so on. Efron (1941) and Ekman and Friesen (1969) have called these gestures "emblems."

The difference between supplemental gestures and emblems is not morphological, but relative to the context. If a demonstrative gesture becomes known in a group, it can henceforth be used *instead of* verbalization, thus becoming emblematic through its usage.

Any gesture can be used to qualify the meaning of speech rather than merely to supplement or replace the verbal representation. In this latter case, gestures are metacommunicative, so I will deal with this idea in Section II. In fact, *gestures are usually metacommunicative*, so I will not discuss them in detail until Section IV.

Other Non-lexical Points

Often a participant will orient his body toward others in a basic posture, then turn his head and address some particular member or some person who has not been included in his basic postural orientation. In such cases he may not perform any activity with his body and hands, but, rather, hold these motionless. Sometimes the converse relation is seen. The body is addressed, and a sequence of non-language behavior is directed, to another person. Meanwhile the head is addressed to some other person but the face is held in deadpan, without expression or speech.

This kind of behavior seems to do several things: It offers

an invitation for encounter to those addressed. It refuses a comment on what is occurring and thereby directs attention elsewhere—to what someone else is saying, for example. And the "contentless" point can maintain mutual orientation in a relationship that is at the moment "inactive."

These various non-language structures, gestures, referencing signals, and "contentless" face, torso, or leg orientations are performed simultaneously. Each is technically a point-unit. Since they are performed simultaneously with different bodily regions, they may constitute simultaneous point-unit elements of a single position. Thus in a single bodily position, a participant uses a complex of point-units —linguistic and otherwise.

A speaker may supplement or replace units of his narrative by a variety of behaviors more complicated than a gesture. He may produce photographs, motion pictures, diagrams, drawings, written descriptions, or sculpture as demonstratives of a point or position.

Units of Task or Actonic Behavior

M. Harris (1964) has described sequences or units of task behavior that he terms "actones." Some of Pike's "behavioremes" are physical tasks of this nature—eating breakfast, for instance (Pike, 1954). Such behaviors may be addressed to physical objects, but they can be addressed to other people in activities such as feeding, lovemaking, and grooming.

In some transactions, the physical task or actonic behavior is featured. People come together *in order* to manufacture a product, to feed, to groom each other, or to prepare a site for a later transaction. In transactions that are explicitly conversational, such actones are intercalated into the stream of language behavior. So people may munch a candy bar, smoke, or adjust the lights or furniture, while they are speaking or listening.

The actonic behavior that appears in a conversation is not necessarily performed in order to inform anyone. It is nevertheless communicative, for its form is often famil-

iar and its significance known. So an actonic behavior may
be used to indicate a meaning. A participant may, for instance, refer to a task or occupation by enacting an actonic
sequence instead of describing the task.

In some cases, emblems are obviously derived from
familiar actonic sequences. Motions of boxing, chopping
actions, drawing the finger across the neck in a simulated
cutting action, or simulating a pistol with the hand are well-
known examples.

The following example shows how, in a therapy session,
actonic acts appeared that were used as signals. Marge, the
young patient, blew her nose, then used the Kleenex as
a signal. She waved to the men with it; then she further
used it as an invitation for contact with Whitaker by drop-
ping it near him on the sofa. He picked it up and handed
it to her.

Whitaker did a somewhat analogous thing in the sequence previously described. He leaned forward and picked
up a minute object from the floor. He played with this
in his hand for the next few minutes, then put it under
Marge's nose and ordered her to smell it.

The act of picking up the object was not simply an element of housekeeping; the object he picked up was used
for a number of minutes in a kind of playing and signaling
behavior, and these sequences terminated in a brief physical contact between Whitaker and the girl.

We could conceive of tactile acts in general as actonic
behaviors that connect participants. McBride (1966) calls
this kind of behavior "bond servicing."

Sometimes elements of courting or sexual behavior are
taken out of context and performed as if they were gestures. In such cases the performer is likely to direct these
behaviors to the attention of a particular other. He may
glance slyly at the object of the display, glance down at
his own exhibited behavior, and so on.

When Marge would change her leg position, she would
rearrange her skirt. As is usual in such behavior, she lifted
her skirt slightly before pulling it down, thus giving the
men a ladylike peek at her legs.

On other occasions, however, Marge exhibited her thighs by allowing her skirts to ride up.[1] And, glancing all the while at Malone, Marge would sometimes stroke her own thighs in slow, writhing movements.

These behaviors are kinesic but they are not the simple gestures that clarify speech. Instead, they are indicative of the larger organization of the group. Such "metabehavior" will concern us in Section IV.

Sometimes activities of different logical types are addressed simultaneously to the same person. Marge, for example, would look at Whitaker and complain of being dead. Simultaneously she would turn her body to him and act courtingly.

In this case, the two behavior sequences differed markedly in the significance of their content. Marge acted sexily, but she spoke a lament, saying she was dead. The messages were actually antithetical.

Notice that two of these behaviors constitute a brief interposed position.[2] Whitaker turned his whole body to Marge at the second contacting and spoke to her as he put his palm under her nose. He used his whole body in picking up the object from the floor. But the other actions, which involved a single bodily region, were carried out with torso and hands, while the participant was also speaking or listening.

In other words, participants use their bodies differentially. *They perform one set of behaviors in one relationship and another set in some other relationship, at the same time.* This was the case in each of the other actonic acts I have described. Thus, for instance, Whitaker picked up

[1] The exhibitionistic leg behavior served to turn the men away from Marge. This is usually the case. The myth is that a woman is seductive if she exhibits thighs beyond the mode of an era or lets her knees drift apart, but observations in any mixed company will show that this behavior regularly causes men to cover their eyes, avert their faces, move back, and turn to someone else for conversation. On the contrary, preening behaviors such as the brief skirt lifting, pressing the calves together, and showing a *little* thigh bring attention *to* a woman.

[2] The remainder of this chapter is excerpted from Chapter 3 of my book *Communicational Structure: Analysis of a Psychotherapy Transaction,* published in 1973 by Indiana University Press. It is reproduced here with the kind permission of the publisher.

Marge's Kleenex, handed it to her, and brushed her hand, without taking his face and eyes away from Mrs. V.

The men lit their pipes without watching what they were doing. They kept listening to Mrs. V. as they did so. Marge did not stop her passive protests or contentions while exhibiting her thighs or using her Kleenex. In the case of the stroking behavior, the lower half of the body was involved, while Marge simultaneously directed her upper body to Malone or the camera, *and* turned her head to address Whitaker.

Thus the body is differentiated in its communicative usage. The head, face, and vocal apparatus are used in one relationship, the upper torso and hands in another; and sometimes the lower body and legs are employed in yet a third relationship.[3] Notice, too, that the activities of these regions are of different logical types. For example, the activities of the head region involve facial expressions and language, which are symbolic actions. The activities of the body and hands can be symbolic when gestures are used, but these actonic behaviors are not symbolic. Such differential activities have led communication theorists to distinguish modalities of communication, or, at the social level, to determine that human communication is multichanneled (Birdwhistell, 1971).

I use these regional differentiations as the first of two bases for distinguishing the subunits of the position. Thus the behavior of the upper or lower body or the head region constitutes one division of positional behavior. The participant who directs his head to one vis-à-vis and his body to another and performs a different kind of sequence in each of these relations is evidencing multiple simultaneous actions in a position. The basic bodily posture of the position is maintained during these differential activities. Thus more than one kind of communicational behavior occurs

[3] Some participants also split their bodily activities along a vertical plane, moving the right side in relation to someone on that side and the left side in another relationship (Scheflen, 1960).

It has been shown experimentally that differences in galvanic skin reflexes between the upper and lower halves of the body on the one hand, and its two sides, on the other hand, correspond to differences in body-image concepts.

LANGUAGE MODALITIES

LINGUISTIC	Lexical or verbal forms (Sapir, 1921; Bloomfield, 1933; Pike, 1954)
	Stress, pitch, and junctures (Sapir, 1921; Joos, 1950; Z. Harris, 1951; Pike, 1954; Austin, 1962)
PARA-LINGUISTIC	Non-language sounds (Trager and Smith, 1956; Trager, 1958; Pittenger and Smith, 1957; Eldred and Price, 1958)
	Vocal modifiers (Pittenger and Smith, 1957; Birdwhistell, 1961; Duncan, 1966)

COMMUNICATIVE BODILY MODALITIES[4]

KINESIC AND POSTURAL FORMS (including movement, facial expression, tonus, positioning, and so on)	(Darwin, 1955; Efron, 1941; Birdwhistell, 1952, 1958, 1960, 1963, 1965, 1966, 1967, 1969; Goffman, 1955, 1961B; Scheflen, 1963, 1964, 1965A, 1965B, 1967, 1968; Ekman and Friesen, 1965, 1967; Hall, 1959; Condon and Ogston, 1966, 1967; Charny, 1966; Kendon, 1967, 1970, 1972; Exline and Winters, 1965)
PARAKINESIC AND POSTURAL QUALITIES	(Birdwhistell, 1969; Mahl, 1966; Berger, 1958; Hewes, 1955; Dittman, 1962; Ekman, 1965)
TACTILE FORMS	(Frank, 1957; Scheflen and Scheflen, 1972)
"ARTIFACTUAL BEHAVIOR"	(including dress, cosmetics, insignia, use of props, and bodily noise)

TABLE 2-1.   A listing of behavioral modalities in communication

---

[4] Birdwhistell has called units of body motion that have a communicative function, "kinesic" behaviors. They appear to have a morphology analogous to that of language; i.e., small elements of movement are successively integrated into larger units (Birdwhistell, 1952, 1960, 1971).

in a single position. Mechanically, the participant positions his body, balances on his buttocks (or on his buttocks and legs), then turns his head in one relation and his body in the other.

Comment: Emic Systems
of Forms
and Meanings

Cultural Specificity

Representational behaviors are not universal in form and meaning; rather, they are culturally specific. A given tradition has a characteristic repertoire of words, gestures, and structural arrangements for the communication of meaning, and the meanings of these behavioral forms are culturally specific. The term "emic" has been used to describe the system of forms and referents used in some given cultural tradition (Pike, 1954, 1957).

Such an emic system is part of the cultural heritage of a society. The members learn the same emic system of forms and meanings. When they come together to communicate a meaning, they use the same system of customary representational forms and thereby make reference to a specific, culturally traditional set of meanings.

The forms of an emic system are learned by the members of a society. As they grow up, people have the opportunity to observe these hierarchical arrangements in their typical form; they also participate in assembling these behaviors, and are told the meanings of representations when they occur. Sometimes they see firsthand the occurrences in relation to their referents.

An individual can experience the contextual referents and learn the system of behaviors used to represent them. And he himself keeps performing the traditional activities, so his children and students are able to learn them. In this way, the customary forms of an emic system are passed on from generation to generation.

The Cognitive Representation of an Emic System

When people become acculturated, they are able to replicate performances of the particular representational hierarchy and meanings of an emic system. They can do this when they are acting within a particular context. They also recall or can imagine a particular context that is not visible and perform the behaviors that traditionally represent that context (see Section II).

Images of behavioral forms and the referents are somehow stored in the central nervous system. On this basis, Miller, Galanter, and Pribram describe how people can plan a course of action. They can imagine a stream of behavior, identify next steps, and imagine the consequences of performing them. Then they can evaluate these expectations, plan a course of action, and take it (Miller, Galanter, and Pribram, 1960). Under certain conditions, a person can perceive or recall a context, imagine a course of action, and activate motor behavior to enact a traditional representational hierarchy.[1] Since the representations of behavior are structured hierarchically, Miller, Galanter, and Pribram (1960) postulated a hierarchical structuring of the cognitive representations of speech, gesture, and the communicative unit. Since the larger communicative units are also customary in structure, these, too, must be represented as mental images. And we could further speculate that these larger units were but subunits in larger and larger units of human behavior that are also represented by cognitive images. As a person enacts a representation in speech or action, he may repeat aloud or

[1] Pribram has postulated that such images may be maintained in circuits that involve oligodendroglia, since these proliferate with learning (Pribram, 1966). Thus Tolman's (1932) idea of cognitive maps has been considerably developed. One can think about such representations in a temporal perspective. Any larger unit or context in a hierarchy extends backward in time from immediate behavior, and it appears to extend forward in time when it is replicated in memory. Thus one can visualize coming events in a pattern. He can imagine and anticipate usual consequences. He can have expectancies (Tolman, 1932; Lewin, 1951; Rotter, 1954); that is, he can image goals, and behaviors necessary to achieve them.

think about the metastatements that are usually made with such an enactment.

One is able to replicate a much more complicated hierarchical *Gestalt* than he can describe in words. A person uses the suprasegmental features of speech, a variety of gestures and facial displays, shifts or "punctuation" behavior, territorial arrangements, and certain regulatory or metabehavior behaviors (see Section II) in exact traditional detail, but he can tell us only about certain gestures and the forms of speech. He cannot apparently visualize the other features. We assume, then, that only certain features of the representational system have been explicated and identified in the history of a people's self-examination. Many features and aspects of an emic system have not been coded in the language of a people, and these are not consciously represented in cognition anywhere in the culture. In addition, of course, there are particular members of that culture who have not learned the known metastatements, and others who have repressed or resisted learning about certain aspects of their behavior. In such cases, the psychoanalysts speak of "mechanisms of defense" (A. Freud, 1946).

The Communicative Properties of a Behavioral Gestalt

A familiar physical structure is communicative.[2] So is a familiar pattern of behavior. Thus, any event is informa-

[2] Any physical form is communicative as long as it is organized as a usual replicate in nature. There is at least some information as long as there is negentropy. Visible physical systems at all levels are patterned and informative.

Groups may have a recognizable configuration of relations. We recognize the form of the human organism by age group, gender, and so on. The form of the DNA molecule is communicative by virtue of the structure of its molecular components. We would also have to include regular non-living structures. We recognize the tools and customary buildings of our culture, for instance.

One can also argue that the difference between a physical and a behavioral system is merely relative. The forms we specify as physical often have a much greater duration than a behavior, but this is not necessarily the case. Some behaviors of an organism are of briefer duration than its physical form, but this is not true of behaviors such as maturation and aging. Organismic form itself is a behavior of systems of genetic and cultural transmission.

tive if it occurs again and again in the same shape and context. Organisms can learn to predict the context whenever the event appears, and they can learn to enact a specific behavioral element to fit into the general context. In addition, people can learn the names of such forms of behavior and can also learn elaborate ideas about the value or significance of such events. Then they can conjure images and talk about these events even when they are not directly perceivable.

If the replications of a meaningful form are to be recognized as members of a common class, however, certain conditions must be met. Each replication must be exact enough and accurate enough for the recurrences to be more like each other than they are like some other kind of behavior. And the replicate must appear each time in its usual or familiar contexts. In the case of language behavior, for instance, where the same forms of speech can be used in a variety of circumstances, we have to perceive the larger *Gestalten* of behavior to tell what a given sound or word means. And, finally, the participants in a transaction must share a common experience of the forms and configurations of behavior if they are to recognize and comprehend each other's actions.

Consider this idea in diachronic, or processual, terms. A participant must make a recognizable *Gestalt* of behavior in order to act communicatively, so he assembles this *Gestalt* step by step. He adds words and maybe sentences until he has depicted an idea. He may also add gestures to clarify abstract concepts. He may display facial sets that further qualify his position. And all of this behavior is carried out in some spot in his total role; he addresses it to someone or to some group of people, and so forth. Eventually, a sufficiently non-ambiguous integration of behavior is assembled so that others can recognize his meaning with a minimum of ambiguity. In Bateson's terms (Bateson, 1972), meaning increases as ambiguity decreases, and ambiguity is decreased by the formation of larger and larger integrations of patterned behavior.

Necessary Conditions for Communicating a Meaning

With these ideas in mind, we can spell out some of the necessary conditions for communicating a meaning:

There must first of all be a workable assemblage of particular kinds of people. The people must have in common the same emic system, and they must come close enough to see and hear each other's enactments and perhaps touch and smell each other. This they can accomplish by using the conventional relational structures described in Chapter Two. But the group must also distance itself from distracting noises and excessive interruptions; it helps to have comfortable furniture and favorable ecological conditions if the communicational process is to take some time. So the group often assembles at a conventional site, prearranged for communication.

Second, one or more group members must assemble a recognizably specific and comprehensive hierarchy of communicative behavior. Using some customary program, the people form reciprocal and complementary relations of positions. In these relations, a person performs certain particular point-units of speech, gesture, or other representational behavior. His complementary partner may add point-units to this performance; the reciprocally related group members may add point-units of listening and comprehension.

It is necessary for the performers to assemble a recognizable *Gestalt* by these efforts. They must add sufficient point-units to specify a given context precisely where there is ambiguity about the matter. Often a presentor will enact a sufficiently complicated hierarchy to depict what is usually, in his experience, a sufficiently specific representation. Then he or others can add specificational enactments as the need arises. In more complicated cases, the meaning may be obscured or contested, and the performance may be questioned, modified, or greatly expanded by group effort. These matters will concern us further in the chapters to come.

Section Two

Contexts: The Structure of Transactions

The communicative unit occurs in a relation of discourse (Chapter Three), in a relationship (Chapter Four), or in an institutional program of activity (Chapter Five).

The communicative acts that make up such a program of activity are called transactions. The meanings and connotations of transactions are the subjects of this Section.

Chapter Three Relations

When two people of Western culture come together for a transaction, they may face each other and act reciprocally, i.e., toward or upon each other; or they may take side-by-side positions and act in a complementary way, i.e., with each other toward some third party or task. In larger groupings, combinations of these two basic arrangements occur. Two side-by-side pairs, for instance, can face each other.

The Vis-à-vis Relation

When two people meet, they will face each other, in a vis-à-vis relation of bodily orientation. More precisely, they use a sequence of vis-à-vis positions, which they orient to each other.

Two people may recognize each other at a distance, exchange a greeting, then turn and walk toward each other. At a customary interpersonal distance they will stop walking, greet again, and take vis-à-vis positions (Kendon and Ferber, 1967).

When participants exchange the "near greeting," they may come within three feet to shake hands or embrace, but they will then assume a distance that falls into either of two major zones (Hall, 1963).

The near, or intimate, distance will ordinarily be less than four feet. Intimate friends and relatives are likely to use this distance, and it is often the distance of face-to-face when only two or three acquaintances talk together. Even strangers may engage at this distance if the area is so noisy that it is difficult to hear each other or if the space is crowded with other people.

The formal distance, of greater than six feet, is likely to be maintained by relative strangers who are engaged in formal relationships. It must also obtain if five or more people are engaged in a circle.

Within the more intimate zone of distance, the actual interpersonal spacing will depend upon ethnicity, the intimacy of the relationship, crowding, and other variables that are interrelated as elements of a system.

In general, northern European-Americans tend to stand about three to four feet apart or just beyond easy tactile range, while eastern European Jewish-Americans and French-Americans tend to stand two and one half to three feet apart, or within easy tactile range. Certain Latin Americans stand at distances of about two feet.

When the two people are involved in an intimate relationship, they are likely to use a full vis-à-vis, facing each other to the exclusion of others. If they are merely acquaintances or are not exclusively involved, they will stand at angles of up to 90 degrees from a full vis-à-vis. This difference is shown in Figure 3-1.

The sites at which transactions are to occur are outfitted with furniture and accessories. In the living room or the

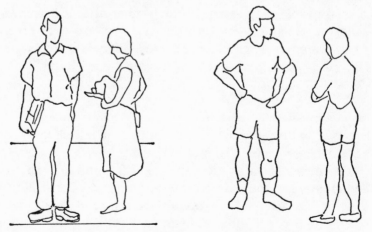

FIGURE 3-1.   Full and 90-degree vis-à-vis relations

meeting room, for instance, chairs and sofas are placed at the usual distances for conversation, and at least some of these seats will face each other to accommodate reciprocal relations. In such cases the main speakers will take face-to-face seats. They will sit down, arrange their clothing and possessions, and address each other. If one participant is awarded the floor without challenge or ambiguity, he may speak from a "relaxed" position, leaning back in his chair with his legs crossed or sprawled in front of him and his hands on the armrests of the chair or folded in his lap. If there are a number of people present and it is not clear who is to speak first, a participant may lay claim to the floor by uncrossing his legs and leaning forward in his seat. He rests the weight of his upper body on his feet and may also protrude and raise his head so that it is held higher than the heads of the other group members. Then he will place one or both hands, or maybe a prop—such as a pencil, a pipe, or a cigarette—in the space immediately in front of him. As he does this, he will address the face of his potential listener or listeners until he has recruited their attention. To aid him in this effort he may clear his throat, cough, or utter a few preliminary paralinguistic sounds.

The relations of posture, orientation, and distance indicate the degree of involvement, intimacy, and type of affiliation of the participants. Variations of this configuration may also indicate the ethnicity and general social position of those who are involved. Finally, the terminal markers and the sequence of enactments provide information about what is to occur next and when it can be initiated. Notice that the postural-kinesic contributions to these configurations are the same acts of positioning and movement that marked the segmentation of the individual enactment.

Side-by-side Relations

Participants who jointly develop a presentation and present it to a third party or a group are likely to stand or sit side by side, as they do when they are watching a performance or engaging in a common physical task.

If the transaction features a central activity, some of the participants may be spectators. In America, at least, spectators tend to station themselves in rows or circles facing the focus of activity. Sometimes rows of seats have been established for the affair, and the spectators will sit side by side in these seats. In other cases they may stand in rows or circles, or seat themselves on the floor or the grass, mutually facing the focus. Thus, spectators are related to each other in a side-by-side arrangement from which they mutually address some more-active performer. Kendon (1969) has observed that spectators are usually stationed in rows for a formal affair and in circles or semicircles for an informal one.

The rings closest to the focus may consist of those who are most closely affiliated with the performers. These people may be relatives of the performers, fellow professionals, or less active participants in the central performance. However, in larger groups, involving professional activities, the membership in rows or rings may be on either a first-come or a status basis.

If there is a temporary lull or intermission in the central activity, the members of spectator rings tend to turn to each other and form *small face-to-face clusters in which conversation occurs*. The people in rows or rings also tend to cluster during the performance. Members who know each other will stand or sit closer to each other than do strangers. In America there is usually a distance of about three or more feet between non-affiliates if the space is not crowded. Affiliates in side-by-side relations will stand at a range from touching to about two feet, unless they are indicating their disaffiliation. Lover-lover affiliations and those of a parent and small children will often maintain tactile contact in such rings by touching shoulders or feet or by holding hands.

When people converse in an open space, they form circles or squares, and some of them will face each other. The members of an established relationship are likely to

remain in side-by-side positions and mutually address third
or fourth parties as if they were spectators in common. I
will describe this arrangement more carefully when seat-
ing positions come under discussion.

If participants are to share in a physical task, they are
likely to sit or stand side by side at a machine or work-
bench, and mutually address the task. If they are seated
in a living room or a meeting room, those who are affiliated
are likely to sit side by side and mutually address other
people.

Those who are strongly affiliated tend to take a side-by-
side position, so we often find a strong tendency for side-
by-side partners to hold a coalition against, or apart from,
others at a gathering. The side-by-side partners may hold
the same point of view and argue in concert against others.
They may resist attempts by other people to engage them
separately. In fact, meeting rooms and living rooms have
prepared side-by-side arrangements of chairs or seats on a
sofa or bench that are often reserved for combinations
who are expected to act in concert. So a sofa may be reserved for lovers, and the side of a table can be held for
the representatives of one nation, company, or school of
thought.

The members of a coalition who share a task or a point
of view are likely to use congruent or parallel postures in
addition to taking seats next to one another. They may sit
back with the right leg crossed over the left and their arms
folded on their chests, for example, and those in agreement
may move at the same time to some other common position. [I have described these arrangements elsewhere in
detail (Scheflen, 1964, 1970). They have also been described by Charny (1966).]

Partners in such a coalition are also likely to move synchronously in their microbehavior. They nod their heads
in synchrony, move their eyes together, and even beat their
feet in the same rhythm. This microsynchrony has been
described in detail by Kendon (1969) and by Condon and
Ogston (1966). Such partners may say the same thing at

the same time, or at least one of them may tend to repeat or echo what the other has said.

Such an arrangement is ritualized in certain transactions. Singers who share a part in harmony sit or stand side by side and use the same posture. Orchestral members who play the same instruments usually sit side by side in a row and move together. Dancers are positioned side by side and move in synchrony. And team members, fellow soldiers, and other affiliates of the same general status are positioned in side-by-side formations when they share a common task.

The partners of a side-by-side may dissociate. They do this by turning slightly away to separate focuses of address and orientation. In such cases they are likely to fall out of congruent postures, but this is by no means always the case. Married partners and close colleagues may turn away from each other to engage in separate conversations but maintain an announcement of affiliation by retaining the same posture. In fact, when they partly dissociate in this way they may add a tactile contact as if to emphasize persistent affiliation at a time of temporary disengagement in one modality.

Stable Relationships

Many relations last for long periods of time or for a lifetime and are sanctioned by institutional forms. Marriage and kinship relations are examples. These relations will be called "relationships."

The members of a stable relationship may turn to face each other and provide reciprocal services when they are alone together, but when they attend a transaction of another institution, they usually act in a complementary way and show certain indications of their established alliance, often by taking side-by-side positions. Here is a brief account of the relatedness often used in such circumstances.

Participants who already know each other will often come to the transaction together. Relatives and colleagues, for example, may arrive in the same conveyance and walk to the site side by side at roughly the same pace. Close affiliates may walk close enough so that their bodies touch, and they may hold hands or put an arm around one other. They will greet other people as a team, and they may walk around the site together, at least until they have established other involvements in the immediate transaction. Kendon (1969) calls side-by-side pairings of this type "mobile withs."

At a fluid transaction in open spaces, subgroupings of people may form for a time, then disband as the participants circulate and form other involvements. Some subgroups of people who are strongly affiliated may remain together in a side-by-side "withness" throughout the transaction. They will walk together, stand at each other's side, and make frequent tactile contact, no matter whom they address. In other cases, the "with" may dissolve as its members become separately involved. However, if the members of a "with" are durably associated—if they are related as spouses, lovers, or close relatives—they will normally reestablish their "withness" from time to time; or they will at least check back with each other at intervals by exchanging a few words, holding one another's gaze for an instant, or establishing a passing tactile contact. Middle-class American marital partners at social engagements tend to reestablish their "withness" about every twenty or thirty minutes by, at least, an exchange of gazes.

Durable affiliations are thus indicated by side-by-side relatedness and tactile contact. In fact, one could assert that people in such relationships are required to indicate the fact if the larger social organization is to be maintained. One can notice that it is somewhat disruptive at a gathering if lovers or married partners act like singles. And it may be difficult to establish order and servicing at a transaction if parents and children do not indicate their affiliation. Partners in a durable affiliation may sometimes conceal their "withness" for some tactical reason, but I think the persistent and habitual omission of such markers in marriage or love relations constitutes a painful and disruptive social deviancy. The disavowal of "withness" by one partner is often strongly experienced by the other as rejection, and is accompanied by feelings of jealousy. As a practicing psychiatrist, I found this to be a common complaint in disturbed marriages, but I was always surprised that the partners who had these difficulties were remarkably unaware of the actual behavioral markers of disaffiliation, such as placing their hands on their faces so as to shut each other out of vision. In extreme cases, partners may actually turn their backs to each other and state a disagreement or a disaffiliation.

Nevertheless, even in such cases of exhibited dissociation, there is a strong tendency for affiliated partners to unwittingly maintain their postural congruence. They may then come into "mirror-imaged parallelism" (Scheflen, 1964). In such a configuration their torsos and heads will be held in matching postures but their extremities will be placed in opposite relations. One, for instance, will have his left leg crossed over the right, while the other, although he also has his legs crossed, has the right leg over the left one. Each may be resting his head on his arm, but one partner is using his left hand while the other is using his right.

In fact, members of an affiliated established relationship may retain isomorphic postures and move in synchrony even when they have actively dissociated by walking away from each other and joining separate groups. One can often observe marital partners or siblings at opposite sides of a large room sitting in the same posture and changing their postures together. In addition, they may be head nodding or gesticulating synchronously even though they are not side by side or even talking to the same *others*. Sometimes these partners will even unconsciously extend their hands or legs toward each other or hold their hands out as if they were holding hands. And later, when these partners compare notes, they are sometimes surprised to find that they were talking about the same things to different listeners. The postural tactile-kinesic indicators of affiliation tend to be persistent, which is necessary in order to maintain social structure in a fluid transaction. Thus, affiliates who indicate disaffiliation stand in sharp contrast to the more usual, though unwitting, behavior of those in coalition.

More-Complicated Communicational Relations

It is unusual to see a simple complementary or reciprocal relation even in a group of only two people. What we actually see in communicational activities is a more complex arrangement of combinations and multiple simultaneous relations among the participants.

If two people are walking around together, they may look ahead of them and maintain a mobile side-by-side "with," without speaking or looking at each other. But they are more than likely to turn their heads to each other from time to time to exchange words. Perhaps they will even sit down from time to time to eat or talk with each other. In this case, they may sit side by side on a bench or a wall and turn their heads to a reciprocal relation.

By the same token, the vis-à-vis relation is likely to "open" from time to time as both participants turn to watch an event of mutual interest. In fact the vis-à-vis relation may open to some extent even while the informing or bond-servicing activities are still in progress. The participants may turn their whole bodies to a 90-degree angle of "awayness," or they may just turn out of a full vis-à-vis with their lower bodies alone. Either or both parties may take their eyes out of the relationship from time to time and search the area or the faces of people in other subgroupings. I believe that such *opening* invites an interruption of the involvement; it is at this point that the group is likely to be joined by a third party (Scheflen, 1964).

Even when two people are alone, it is usual for one or both of them to refuse a total body vis-à-vis. They are likely to avoid a complete involvement by directing their torsos or their legs away from each other. In some cases one arm is hung over the arm of the chair and dangled away from the other person. The dissociated arm will not be moved in harmony with the rest of the body. One often gets the impression in observing such behavior that this arm or maybe one leg is directed to some imaginary third person. It is not unusual for one or both parties to turn occasionally to an empty chair or space and address an eye orientation and a sequence of remarks to this vacant location.

So even when only two people are involved with each other, they are likely to hold some other involvement as well, and thus not engage each other totally. Thus each may converse and maybe even touch, but each may cast glances outside their twosome. Or they may face each other, but project their voices for others to hear. And it is similarly characteristic for participants to turn into and out of reciprocal relations as they continue together. Thus, the degree of mutual involvement waxes and wanes, and with these fluctuations the twosome is opened and closed to other people.

When a group of spectators are watching a focus, they will be lined up in side-by-side relations. But when there is a lull or intermission, they may turn to each other and form face-to-face groupings for conversation. Therefore, the arrangement may alternate between small-group, vis-à-vis arrangements and lines of side-by-side relations. In fact, this tendency for a larger group to break into multiple small groups which then reunite is characteristic of transactions that last an hour or more.

During intermissions or in transactions in which there is no staged activity, the people may wander around singly or in mobile "withs" and form temporary small groups for greeting and conversation. In groups of three or more people there may be one or even multiple interactional axes (Goffman, 1963).

In the first instance, two people will take up a vis-à-vis relation, and subordinates or members of their "with" will take positions beside these two principals. Thus two side-by-side relations may confront one another. In other cases, when there are more than two main figures and more than two preaffiliated "withs," the participants may form a triangle, square, or small circle. In this case, the dominant figures will be nearly equidistant from each other. Less-dominant members, children, and less-active participants in a "with" may step back a little from the main configuration. There will also be a number of interactional axes as various members of the small group turn their bodies or heads and address each other.

In such a grouping each speaker will rotate his address from one listener to another so that all are included. If he does not do this, those group members who are ignored will tend to drift away or begin subordinate reciprocals. This often happens, of course, so that one primary, or principle, involvement develops. If this happens, some participants may drift into a side-by-side relation with a principle protagonist and establish a new complementary "with." In turn, members of a side-by-side "with" may turn and address each other to re-establish their relationship or recalibrate their joint enactment.

Thus, side-by-side listeners may glance at each other if they are uncertain about the implications of a speaker's enactment. If they have to discuss their stand, they will turn face to face to do so. If they disagree temporarily, partners who are strongly affiliated may establish a tactile contact during the interval of their disagreement.

People who have to co-ordinate their specialized share of an enactment will glance at each other and exchange words or kinesic signals, though they sometimes do this tactilely. And whatever other parts the participants are taking, they can often be seen to share gazes, brief face-to-face interchanges, or tactile holds to maintain, reaffirm, or repair their affiliation.

The particular nature of the relationship, then, influences the structure of their enactments. They indicate by these postural, orientational, and tactile relations both their temporary or programmatic relations and their pre-established and durable ones. They organize time and space by their relations of orientation and interpersonal distances, as well as indicate their interruptibility. Thus, we can speak of behavioral—as well as fixed and prearranged—territoriality.

It is not typical in a larger group any more than in a dyad for the participants to be totally engaged with a single other person or "with." From his standing or seated base, each participant can separately orient his different bodily regions and engage with several others at the same time.

Two people may be talking to each other. Each of them may have side-by-side partners who are listening while engaged in casting glances at each other. Any of these people may be exchanging glances and facial activities with people outside the immediate subgrouping. Various tactile connections may exist among these participants, and some of the participants may be simultaneously engaged in actonic performances which others watch and occasionally expedite.

In this way, participants can engage in transient reciprocals or alliances while maintaining other relationships, and they can carry out multiple-featured and supplementary enactments at the same time. Elsewhere I have described instances of such multiple relatedness in detail (Scheflen, 1973).

In each of the multiple relations of a transaction, certain forms of behavior may be shared. Thus, we can speak of multiple channels of communication (Birdwhistell, 1971). There will be relations of face-sharing and gaze-sharing, and relations of speech content and speech tone or vocal qualities. There will also be a variety of possible tactile relations, a number of kinds of kinesic interchanges, and an interpersonal distance. We can think, then, of this variety of communicational exchange as "contents," which can occur within the postural orientational structures of side-by-side and face-to-face relations.

However, we know that the type of interchange will be constrained by the program of activities and the rules of conduct for social relationships. Thus, a variety of interchanges could occur in any channel, but only certain of these are allowable in a given context.

Only certain things are supposed to be verbalized at given occasions among people of certain relationships. We are not, for example, supposed to touch certain kinds of other people, or else we are allowed to touch them only on the shoulder or elbow. On occasion it may be unwise to take a reciprocal position at all with a member of another "with," but when we do so, it may be necessary to avoid gaze-holding, tactile contact, and distances of less than four feet.

I could not begin to outline here the rules of communicative conduct even for those cultures and transaction types that we have studied in detail. But we do know that they are traditional by culture, institution, and activity and that they are known consciously or otherwise by adequately acculturated members of that background. Therefore, such people can enact them in customary and recognizable ways, and all participants of that background can recognize these configurations when they occur. Thus they can know at a glance the range of possible relationships that obtain, as well as the range of activities that are probably occurring.

By arrangements like this, complex depictions may be assembled, questioned, explained, explored, and elucidated by complicated communicational processes. By the same token, of course, a meaning may be obscured or confounded.

Chapter Four

Interactions

When two or more people come together, they engage in a common activity such as conversation or courtship. This activity forms a context for the relations, which become phases in the sequences of the activity. Each phase is a context for the particular kinds of communicative behavior that each participant contributes. Three kinds of activities will be described in this chapter: discourse, courtship, and quasi courtship.

Units of Discourse

We can describe units of speech behavior as I have done in Chapter One only when we examine the behavior of one participant at a time. But communicational units ordinarily occur at the social level. Units of representational behavior, then, will include the behavioral contributions of all members.

Ordinarily a speaker orients his body and face to his auditors, and in this position he makes his point. It may be a speech unit, a gesture, an actonic demonstration, or all of these simultaneously. In face-to-face conversations, the orientation of middle-class Americans is rarely eye to eye. Each fixates his central vision at a spot somewhere between the cheek and the shoulder of the other fellow, just out of the range for eye-to-eye gazing. When central vision is focused on the cheek-shoulder area of a vis-à-vis, the remainder of the upper body is visible in peripheral vision. When movement occurs outside the space, it will be perceived in peripheral visual fields and will trigger an orienting reflex. Focal vision is then shifted to observe the moving part.

The accuracy of an orientation is worthy of comment. In an audience of forty or fifty people a speaker can "point" his head and eye convergence with sufficient accuracy to single out one auditor. This object of attention usually is aware that he is being addressed. Similarly, we can project our voices accurately enough to evoke a response from one person in a group—sometimes even if this person is behind us. With reasonably high-resolution motion pictures and a little practice, an observer can tell visually which participants are addressing each other. The interested reader should become acquainted with the careful experimental studies of Kendon on gaze in interaction (Kendon, 1965).

A listener may sit forward in his chair if he is contending for the floor or if he is of appreciably lower status, but he often sits back and addresses his eyes and face in the general direction of the speaker. A dominant listener may look the speaker fully in the face, but more often he looks just to the speaker's left or right, and he may look down if he is under criticism or look up to the ceiling, as speakers do, to indicate thoughtfulness.

Listeners are constrained at least to appear attentive. This they may do by remaining generally silent except for occasional questions or comments. They may also cock their heads to bring one ear closer to the speaker, and sometimes they point to their ear by placing their hand on the side of the jaw and extending an index finger. Sometimes listeners may even cup a hand behind an ear. In addition, they may adopt a bland and thoughtful countenance. However, listeners are also supposed to render comprehension signals from time to time. Head nodding is one way to do so, but equally successful are smiling and laughing at appropriate times, and supplying other demeanors appropriate to the speaker's statements. Some listeners fall into synchronous hand gestures and head movements with speakers—a behavior that often consists in supplying the same hand, head, and eye markers that the speaker is using (Condon and Ogston, 1966; Kendon, 1968; Scheflen, 1970).

Actually, listeners perform point-units. Many of these consist merely in reorienting their face-eye address with that of the speaker, without speaking.

Psychotherapists tend to minimize their activity in listening. They hold a dead pan and minimize comprehension signals, for example. Whitaker and Malone did this, but not as markedly as some therapists do. In their positions of listening and questioning, they performed as follows: They cocked their heads slightly and addressed Mrs. V. They suppressed virtually all body movement and facial expression in the dead pan that psychotherapists deliberately use to minimize influence on the speaker. They would occasionally *signal attentiveness:* lean the head forward; cock it, turning the ear; and use an overwide position of the eyelids.

But listeners may interrupt their silence and ask brief questions without abandoning the listening position. Whitaker, for example, repeatedly asked questions. He would extend his neck so that his head was high, jutted forward, and slightly cocked. He would direct his face, gaze, and eye focus to the addressee (Marge or Mrs. V.), and take his pipe out of his mouth and hold it forward. He would then articulate the question. At its termination he would raise his head still farther, jut his jaw slightly, and raise his eyebrows until an answer was begun. Then he would lower and retract his head and return his pipe to his mouth.

Modes of Reciprocal Speaking

Reciprocal speakers tend to look at each other's face in narratives. They do not, however, look in one another's eyes except in a direct, aggressive confrontation or in a sexual, courting exchange. If, in a group of males, one of greatly higher status or dominance is addressing the others, he may look directly at their faces even when he is listening. It is as though dominant males and those awarded the temporary status of speaker have charge of the gazing space directly in front of their faces.

However, speakers do not always look at the faces of their listeners. They may look down at their feet if they are speaking tentatively or hesitantly and at times when they subjectively report shame, guilt, or a fear of offending. The position of "head down" is sometimes a posture of submissiveness.

A speaker may also look upward, over the head of his listener. When he does so, he is likely to jut his jaw and bring his lower lip over the upper. He may even rub his chin or scratch the back of his head. Such posturing indicates thoughtfulness and may be associated with the subject's feeling of wishing to think about what he will say.

These forms of speaking address are associated with differences in voice projection, eye convergence, muscle tone, and paralanguage. In the usual mode of intimate or personal conversation, the eyes are converged appropriately for the distance between participants and the voice is projected directly to the listener. Birdwhistell (1963) calls this the interpersonal mode.

When the face and eyes are addressed to the floor, the speaker is likely to underproject the voice almost to inaudibility, and he may assume a hunched shoulder posture and a sagging of the musculature in general. When he speaks while looking over or beyond the shoulder of his listener, he is likely to converge his eyes at a point past the listener and overproject his voice outward to the "world at large." In this case, a speaker may bring back his shoulders and protrude his chest, and he may also lean backward and hold his head high. Birdwhistell (1963) calls these two modes, respectively, the intrapersonal and the extrapersonal.

In the simplest reciprocal relations, a speaker assembles a sequence of representational statements to which others indicate their comprehension or the lack of it by nodding, making facial displays, and commenting. The speaker may maintain his narrative position as he observes these indications, adding further point-units of speech or illustrations if these seem necessary.

In more formal presentations, time may be saved for

questions, discussion, or rebuttal. A common format in Western meetings is a presentation, followed by several periods of comment, and then a period of debate or discussion. More-complex formats are, of course, in use. Some provide for the exposition of a variety of viewpoints, and others make use of an agenda that permits a number of topics or matters to be brought up sequentially.

The role of speaker may also change hands. One person may take a position of narration for a while as the others listen; then another participant may take the floor and state a different position. This arrangement is characteristic of dialogue and negotiation.

If the utterance of one participant seems to elicit a response or a counterstatement from another participant, the sequence has an action-reaction format. If the first person then responds to what the second has said, a more complex sequence of interaction occurs (Menninger, 1958; Colby, 1960; Bales, 1950).

In fact, however, the structure of an interaction is governed by customary rules and agenda. Participants often take turns speaking according to such agenda, paying little or no heed to each other's statements, so interaction is minimal. Only the timing of their utterances is interactional. On other occasions, people do pay attention to each other, but the range of topics and ideas is governed by the agenda of the transaction. In this case the program of conversation follows the model of a game in which moves are contingent upon each other, but the allowable kinds and ordering of moves are governed by the rules.

Courtship Reciprocals

Some of the common activities of early courtship in America are courtship readiness, positioning for courtship, and actions of appeal or invitation.[1] Courtship behaviors

[1] This section, on courting displays, and the next section, on quasi courting, are reprinted from an article by the author called "Quasi-Courting Behavior in Psychotherapy." This article was printed in *Psychiatry* 28:245–57 (August 1965). This excerpt from that article is republished here with the kind permission of the William Alanson White Foundation, Inc.

occur after a participant has reached a specific state of readiness. People in high courtship readiness are often unaware of it and, conversely, subjects who think they "feel" very sexually active often do not evidence courtship readiness at all. Courtship readiness is most clearly evidenced by a state of high muscle tone. Sagging disappears, jowling and bagginess around the eyes decrease, the torso becomes more erect, and pot-bellied slumping disappears or decreases. The legs are brought into tighter tonus, a condition seen in "cheesecake" and associated with the professional model or athlete. The eyes seem to be brighter. Some women believe their hair changes. Skin color varies from flush to pallor—possibly depending upon the degree of anxiety. It is possible that changes in water retention and odor occur.

Preening often accompanies these organismic changes, sometimes only as token behaviors. Women may stroke their hair, or glance at their makeup in the mirror, or sketchily rearrange their clothing. Men usually comb or stroke their hair, button and readjust their coats, or pull up their socks. Some preening behaviors that have been observed in psychotherapy sessions are shown in Figure 4-1.

After the earliest steps, the courting partners assume

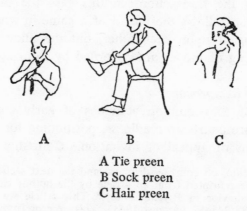

A   B   C

A Tie preen
B Sock preen
C Hair preen

FIGURE 4-1.   Some preening behaviors of male psychotherapists

postures that have a standard relationship. The partners turn their bodies and heads so as to face each other in a vis-à-vis or tete-à-tete configuration. They tend to lean toward each other and place their chairs or extremities in such a way as to block off others. Figure 4-2 shows the vis-à-vis positioning used in courtship. It also depicts the courtship position used when the parties open the position of the upper half of their bodies to include a third person, but form a closed circle with their legs. When courting partners orient themselves vis à vis and come into closer physical proximity, they usually adopt an intimate mode of conversation.

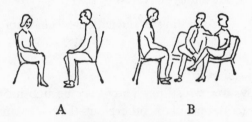

A

B

A With two people
B With third party present

FIGURE 4-2.   Positioning for courtship

The assumption of one participant of a vis-à-vis orientation with courtship readiness may be considered an invitation to court or to related activities. Other activities also appear to invite reciprocation in courtship. In addition to complementary or invitational statements and soft or drawling paralanguage, characteristic bodily motions are seen. Flirtatious glances, gaze holding, demure gestures, head cocking, rolling of the pelvis, and other motions are well known. In women, crossing the legs, slightly exposing the thigh, placing a hand on the hip, and exhibiting the wrist or palm are invitational. Protruding the breast and slow stroking motions of the fingers on the thigh or wrist also are common. Some of these activities, seen in psychotherapy sessions, are illustrated in Figure 4-3.

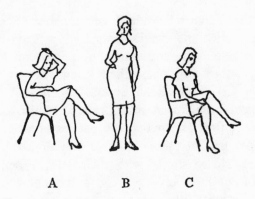

A   B   C

A Presenting the palm, with hair preening
B Rolling the hip
C Presenting and caressing the leg

FIGURE 4-3.   Appealing or invitational behaviors of women patients

Quasi Courtship

Two boys are wrestling. They may be fighting for domination or to defeat each other, but they also may have a quite different purpose. Their wrestling may not, even over years of repetition, progress to victory for either boy. Neither is hurt or humiliated. Instead of showing anger, both may laugh and show evidence of considerable pleasure. None of the spectators even thinks of intervening. They seem to know from the beginning that injury and victory are not the aims of this interaction. Or two men approach each other in a barroom. They call each other the vilest names, exchange mock punches, then embrace and buy each other drinks. Animals also show such mock fighting (Bateson, 1955). Two dogs may rush at each other with such a show of ferocity that a spectator would expect them to tear each other apart; instead they romp off gaily together in play.

In such situations, two sets of behavior seem to be alike, but some signal occurs that lets those who know the rules distinguish between them. Some indication occurs that the activity is not a real fight; it is not to be taken literally.

Partners in a quasi courtship may make references to

the inappropriateness of the situation for sexuality by reminding each other that other people are present or by
reminders of taboos or ethical considerations. They may
also remind each other that they are together to conduct
the business at hand. In psychotherapy, the patient may
be encouraged to feel her sexual feelings fully; yet she may
be cautioned, by reference to the context, not to act them
out. More often than not, such references are non-verbal.
A gesture or a movement of the eyes or head toward the
setting or toward others is as effective as any verbal statement about inappropriateness.

After the earliest steps in a courtship, the partners move
into vis-à-vis relationship of posture and adopt an intimate
mode of conversation, excluding others from their relationship. In quasi courtship the relationship of postures is
incomplete. The participants may face each other but turn
their bodies so that they face partly away from each other,
or they may extend their arms so as to encompass others.
Or they may cast about the room with their eyes or project
their voices so as to be clearly audible to third parties. This
story of divided loyalties is told in Figure 4-4. In Figure

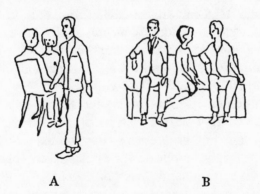

A   B

FIGURE 4-4.   Multiple postural relationships in quasi courting

4-4A the woman, in vis-à-vis positioning with a man, turns
in search behavior to another man, passing by. In Figure
4-4B, the couple on the right are in a semiclosed tete-à-
tete position, but the woman is touching the other man

with her ankle. This kind of division of the body in multiple simultaneous relationships, we have called splitting.

The behaviors may be modified so as to leave out characteristic courting elements. This is done by failing to complete typical courting actions or by conducting them only in certain communicative modalities so that the *Gestalt* required for a courting unit is not completed. For example, in courtship a man may lean forward, touch his partner, soften his facial expression, and, in soft paralanguage, verbalize his love. In quasi courting he may say the words while leaning slightly away from her, smile only by retracting the corners of his lips without crinkling his eyes, and use a matter-of-fact tone of voice.

Participants in quasi courting may try to reduce ambiguity and indicate non-courtship by lexical disclaimers. They may reassure the partners and others that their interest is not sexual. They may seem to court while talking about their love for another partner, or they may intellectualize the flirtation in a discussion, say, of great books.

It is logical that quasi-courting forms might differ between the classes, since their dating and courtship patterns are known to differ markedly. There is an American middle-class tendency to combine romantic love, which historically was a platonic concept, with active sexuality. It may be this combination that necessitates signals for differentiating courting and quasi courting. Qualifiers seem to be learned by middle-class children first in their relations with older relatives and later in the characteristic middle-class dating pattern with its ritualistic flattery, dance programs, and non-progressing courtshiplike routines. But the non-upwardly mobile lower class, which separates romantic love and sexuality, has not developed a dating pattern of this kind and apparently lacks the pattern of quasi courting well known in the middle class.[2]

[2] For discussions of middle-class dating patterns, see the following: D. D. Bromley and F. H. Britten, *Youth and Sex: A Study of 1300 College Students* (New York: Harper, 1938); Rayanne D. Cupps and Norman S. Hayner, "Dating at the University of Washington," *Marriage and Family Living* 9, 30–31 (1947); Winston Ehrmann, *Premarital Dating Behavior* (New York: Holt, 1959); C.

In the traditionbound performances in a culture, a relatively few elemental units of behavior serve as basic building blocks for constructing complex and variegated patterns. An integration as complex as a long discourse, for example, is based upon a relatively small number of standard phonemes. In English, only forty-three such elements make up the thousands of morphemes (similar to words), which in turn are formed into such complex structures as sentences, conversation, and literature. In an analogous way, a few elements of courting behavior are put together in the complex pattern of courtship; these same elements, arranged in a different way and combined with "qualifiers," make up integrations that resemble courtship but have a quite different significance in an interaction.

Since quasi courting contains courtship elements, it is tempting to say that quasi courting is no more than aim-inhibited courtship. This idea is misleading, implying that interactants want to court or seduce and are merely dissuaded by circumstances or inhibition. On the contrary, quasi courting is a distinct element in American middle-class culture, learned separately and earlier than courtship and having a very different function. Once this situation has evolved, whatever the origins of quasi courting, a person "knows" at some level of consciousness that quasi courting elicits different behavior from courting. He can therefore intend to "quasi court" from the beginning of the relationship, and his behavior does not necessarily have to be attributed to any other intent.

Quasi courting is a complex of behaviors that resembles courtship. It can be distinguished from actual courtship by three major characteristics: (1) the integration of components, in which qualifiers state, in essence, "This activity is not to be taken literally as seduction"; (2) the contexts of appearance: quasi courting occurs in contexts in which

Kirkpatrick and T. Caplow, "Courtship in a Group of Minnesota Students," *American Journal of Sociology* 51, 114–25 (1945); Robert T. Ross, "Measures of the Sex Behavior of College Males Compared with Kinsey's Results," *Journal of Abnormal and Social Psychology* 45, 753–55 (1956); Geoffrey Gorer, *The American People: A Study in National Character* (New York: Norton, 1948).

courting or sexual behavior is inappropriate; (3) the ulti-
mate progression of the behaviors in the interactional sequence determines whether the pattern is one of courtship
or quasi courtship. The quasi-courtship pattern does not
proceed to sexual consummation even in the later history
of a given relationship.[3]

It is possible to postulate a state of quasi-courting readiness that includes a few aspects of courtship readiness but
is observably different. For example, women may imitate
the appearance of high muscle tone of courtship readiness
by wearing nylon hose and high-heeled shoes, which throw
the foot into flexion and tighten the hamstrings; or they
may adopt a particular type of provocative, slightly bizarre
attire and cosmetics, which give the impression of "sexi-
ness." Such devices appear to solicit quasi courting rather
than courting, and experienced men recognize that "sexy"
women are not necessarily sexual.

Quasi courting occurs in nearly any situation—at least
among the middle class—in which the members know each
other and are engaged in a common objective. The sequence can be observed in the classroom, dining room,
and meeting hall, and between parents and children, hosts
and guests, teachers and students, and doctors and patients.
It occurs between men and women and between people of
the same gender. The intensity and duration vary from the
briefest of kinesic interchanges (in formal activities such
as psychotherapy) to the most elaborate, continuous, and
intense rituals in situations such as the cocktail party. In
the upper-middle-class social context, in fact, quasi courting takes on the quality of a deliberate game for enhanc-
ing attractiveness and social interest. Quasi courting across
marital lines is common. It does not produce signs of anxiety or force interruption so long as certain rules are ob-

[3] This is why there is a serious risk of misinterpreting component
behaviors of any pattern when they are observed out of context. If,
for example, you hear only that two men exchanged kisses, without
knowing that the context was a French military ceremony, you might
wrongly interpret the kissing as homosexual. This is the shortcoming
of the currently popular isolation-of-variables method of research,
in which this or that element of behavior is studied as an isolated
phenomenon.

served. Of course, the alarm bell rings when one party begins excluding others by seeking isolation.

Often, a quasi-courting relationship is at some point converted into an actual courtship. I have no observational data on this eventuality, but I would guess that some special signals or statements would be required to indicate the transition. On the other hand, a courtship may at some point be converted into a quasi courtship. This would be indicated by the addition of the qualifiers. But, by and large, in a quasi-courting sequence, the qualifiers are enacted from the beginning.

The occurrence of any deviance highlights and clarifies the lawfulness of the normal structure. For instance, an interactant may perform courting when it is inappropriate to do so, or perform overly intense quasi courting as a means of forcing another participant to withdraw from the relationship. Or the qualifiers may be deliberately kept unclear in order to produce an ambiguity between courtship and quasi courtship, thereby confusing the other participant or forcing him to declare his intentions.

Courtship displays are used, of course, in courtship, marriage, and certain other institutional procedures. Stylistic variants of these behaviors are employed in the theater and in modeling. Other stylized variants are used in prostitution and still others in homosexual relationships.

But most institutional procedures prohibit the use of full courtship reciprocals. Instead they employ quasi-courting variants. These presumably foster and maintain reciprocality during the transaction and from transaction to transaction in the institution. A particular quasi-courting variant, called rapport, is fostered and employed in psychotherapy. Another variant, flirting, is often used at social engagements for a variety of purposes. But some form of quasi courting is generally used in institutional proceedings of any duration in which men and women are both engaged.

Chapter Five

Institutional Programs

We can observe, in an institution, transactions or communicational units still more complicated than positions, units of discourse, or relations. The transaction is the largest unit in the hierarchy of immediate contexts.

The form and sequencing of units in any customary transaction is governed by a traditional program or agenda.

Arrangement for an Institutional Transaction

The transactions of an institution are ordinarily held at a prearranged site on particular occasions. This site may be a building of a characteristic appearance and construction. Some room in the building may be used for given transactions; it is likely to be laid out and decorated in a certain way. The décor often includes the special symbols, colors, and iconic or graphic representations of that institution, and the furniture or machinery is likely to be of a particular type and arrangement. To one who is familiar with the institutional procedures, these arrangements may be clearly recognizable and identifiable. Thus participants and observers know what is to occur there and how it is usually interpreted. On other occasions the site is not prearranged, but given transactions usually call for particular kinds of places, which are selected and structured by at least the groupings of the members.

The transactions of an institution are attended by particular people and established groups of people. These people have status relationships which may determine their location at the site. They are also likely to take particular configurations of orientation and distance, so the social structure may also identify the transaction and the institution in which it occurs.

The procedure of an institutionalized transaction will be governed by a traditional program. Such a program of behavior might be described as follows: In the structural observation of a transaction, we notice that at any moment of time some gross configuration of relations is occurring. Within this arrangement, a number of different subrelations can be seen, and in each of these some visible or audible interchange, or complementarity of enactments, is occurring.

However, at any moment, at any level of integration, these relations may change. Joe stops talking and shifts his gaze from Bill to Mary, or Mary turns 90 degrees and comes into side-by-side relationship with Bill, or Bill and Mary leave that group and engage elsewhere. If we will observe these changes in relation over and over in a given type of transaction, we will discover that their sequencing is highly regular or customary from one occurrence of that transaction to the next. There are set stages to most transactions; the sequencing is governed by physical, logical, and traditional considerations. In a customary transaction there are prescribed relations and conjoint enactments, so I will say that the structure of communication in the transaction is *programmed*.

If an agreed-upon definition of the situation is attained, the transaction proceeds through its customary steps toward a point of completion. When a stated goal is achieved, or can clearly not be achieved, the group will disband or begin another type of transaction.

When a subtask is completed or the situation is defined, a new set of activities may be taken up, and a different distribution of bodily regions, relations, and relationships will often occur at this point of shift. Thus, a transaction has clear-cut stages, which can be discovered and described, with careful observation. At any phase, there will be one or more main activities and a number of supplementary or intercalated sequences to maintain or change the states of the participants, their relationships, and the ecology of the situation.

Some transactions are rigidly programmed. Each step must be performed in exactly the same order each time, and a stereotyped enactment must be carefully reproduced. But ordinarily a range of alternatives and variations are allowed, some of which are prescribed and considered necessary.

There are a number of ways the transaction can be carried out. It may not matter who takes the various parts nor how the relations are composed, as long as the various tasks are advanced or completed. In other transactions, limits may be placed on the variations and alternatives, but, nevertheless, a number of alternatives are permitted. In still other cases, the use of certain alternative arrangements may be customarily prescribed to adapt the performances to certain contingencies.

In some organizations, a short form of the business meeting is used when a guest is present or entertainment is planned. There are alternatives in many programs to fit the weather conditions at the time of the performance. In many transactions, program variants are called for when certain members do not attend.

In any event, a customary program will have some range of usual and allowable alternative procedures and steps. The same variability holds for the styles of performance that are allowable. In some cases, only skilled performers are allowed to participate. In others, all participants must be middle class, native born, or otherwise fit a mold, so a wide range of dialects and styles is not permitted. Many transactions prescribe a given demeanor and moods, so variants in facial expression, vocal qualities, and rate of movement are not tolerated, but in other transactions the health, mood, regional origins, religion, or ethnicity of the participants is unimportant, so a wide range of styles is observable.

The other constraints and allowances for variation are traditional. They are established by custom for that transaction. In some cases, however, constraints are enforced by particular participants or groups, or they may become necessary because of situational factors that demand a rapid and expert performance. On the other hand, various circumstances may order the repeal of usual constraints. If one participant is sick, angry, or a foreigner, for instance, his enactment may be allowed even though it differs markedly in form and style.

In some cases, the program provides that the transaction shall proceed along established lines until some circumstance is encountered. Then a given course of events is to be chosen and decided upon or even innovated.

A transaction may be exploratory: a situation is looked into by customary routes or methods of exploration, and then the subsequent course of events is determined by what is found. In transactions for solving problems, the program may provide that after a given point *no usual* steps can be taken. Thus, new steps have to be improvised or innovated (Miller, Galanter, and Pribram, 1960).

The program may also prescribe a reciprocation, so the outcome will hinge upon what one or more people do. Their range of choices may be limited, however, by usual rules of etiquette and conduct (Goffman, 1959) or by specific rules for that game. Negotiations and games are programmed in this way.

Certain provisions are usually made for disruptive contingencies, and priority is given to intercalated enactments that customarily meet these contingencies. Priority may be given for the intercalation of an actonic sequence that prevents interruption and interference and maintains the necessary ecology at the site. Priority may also be given for necessary activities of bond servicing or organismic servicing if these threaten the ability of members to continue their performance. Alternative courses of action and substitutable variants have usually evolved to adapt the performances to contingencies that cannot be contained or prevented. All the participants may stop what they are doing and share in these necessary operations.

Innovations and other non-customary enactments or relations do, of course, occur in any performance of a traditional program. Individuals find better ways to enact a part, and these may be incorporated to form a cultural innovation, but I doubt if innovativeness is as common as we imagine. Often, what is novel to the observer is already an established practice in some division of culture that the observer is too inexperienced to know about.

More frequently, an enactment or relation is borrowed from some other program or some other tradition. This non-customary enactment is introduced from misconception or an attempt to change the activities and relationships that are in progress.

In many cases, the other participants allow a non-programmatic occurrence to pass unnoticed, or they ignore it if an explanation or apology is made and the performers resume doing what is expected. But certain non-programmatic performances and relations will be actively disallowed. The progression of the transaction will stop while others criticize, expel, punish, or instruct the offenders. In some such cases, the unacceptable enactment or relation is simply inappropriate to the definition of that situation. In others it is deviant; that is, unallowable by the rules of conduct anywhere in that cultural tradition.

The psychotherapy session exemplifies this point. A customary program constrains and shapes the lexical interchanges and the formation of rapport. Distinctive postural arrangements obtain at each stage of the session, and shifts in these arrangements mark the end of one stage and the beginning of the next. Therapists use a sequence of postures associated with the progression of their tactics of intervention on the patient's behalf.

Most obvious of these relations between tactics and posture is the shift by the therapist from leaning backward with arms or legs crossed to leaning forward with arms and legs uncrossed when he stops listening and starts interrupting, confronting, or reassuring. The subjective experience of rapport also occurs in connection with the assumption of a characteristic pattern of postures. The shifts of the program of a psychotherapy hour move toward the rapport constellation, which in a sense is a "climax." In sessions of about forty minutes' duration, this usually develops at about the twentieth to the twenty-fifth minute. Then, as in most of the sessions we have studied, the entire series is repeated.

There may be a progression of units at various levels in a program; an orderly sequence of maneuvers, for instance, which make up a larger tactic. The tactics, in turn, have an order. The postures of the therapist indicate or mark these progressions of maneuvers and tactics. For example, maneuvers can be equated with points, which are indicated by head-eye postures. Tactics can be equated with

1 Progressive uncrossing of extremities

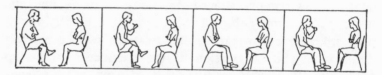

2 Progressive movement toward the patient

Less conventional progression, leading to physical contact

FIGURE 5-1.   Types of progressions of therapists' positions.[1] The first two series of progressions are typical of psychoanalytically oriented psychotherapists, while the last progression illustrates less conventional progression, leading to physical contact.

[1] Reprinted from an article by the author (Scheflen, 1964). This drawing is reprinted here with the kind permission of the William Alanson White Foundation, Inc.

positions, which are marked by total body posture. A progression of tactics (positions) characteristically seen in psychotherapy sessions of any type is illustrated in Figure 5-1. The progressive uncrossing of extremities and movement toward the patient—with or without physical contact—are combined, and each shift is followed by increased clinical activity and lexical engagement, such as interpretation, reassurance, or instruction.

This progressional posture does *not* occur when the interaction with a patient is not a therapeutic session—for example, a demonstration interview for students, or a consultation in which the therapist is examining another psychiatrist's patient. In psychoanalytic language, the therapist in these situations does not encourage transference.

According to the level of behavior, postures indicate the beginnings and endings of units of communicative behavior, the ways in which participants are related to each other, and the steps in a program. Although research has so far only sketched broad outlines of communicative behavior, it is already possible to use this information in clinical practice and everyday life. The briefest glance at postural configurations has great value in identifying the participants' location in a flow of social events and the nature of their relationships. An example of postural sequencing appears in Figure 5-1.

The Place of Meanings

A program prescribes a sequence of physical task operations, a representation of the beliefs of an institution, or both of these. Sometimes such representation seems almost incidental to the performance of the transaction.

In some actonic procedures, for instance, the communication of meaning does not play a central role. The people assemble and carry out a set of operations to make a product. They may think about and occasionally affirm aloud the standards of performance and the values of the product, but this kind of communicational activity may not be a necessary part of *each* transaction.

In other transactions, the program *features* the communication of institutional meanings, as in the case of the Mass. In a religious institution, for example, the meanings are continuously reaffirmed, and certain of the transactions of educational institutions are devoted to the explanation of meanings. Theatrical and musical performances also feature the replication of meaning.

The Mass is a case in point.

The program calls for members of the Church to assemble at a given building at certain times of the week. This building has been elaborately prepared for the holding of the Mass. The seats are arranged in a certain way. The building itself may be laid out in the form of the Cross, and crosses decorate the room and many items within it.

The sign of the cross is a good example of the specialized connotations that have been assigned in Christianity to the wooden frame the Romans used for crucifixion. The entire issue of martyrdom is represented by this stylized symbol, as, in fact, is the total belief system of Christianity. In turn, the Cross can be represented by an emblematic gesture.

Particular people are supposed to come to the Mass, though others are allowed to attend. These people take certain seats in the church. They often arrange themselves in side-by-side groupings according to their kinship relationships. All the members face the altar, at which several participants in special dress carry out specialized activities.

The activities of the Mass are programmed by the liturgy, which has often been described. In essence, a series of steps are prescribed at which certain meanings are represented and ritualistically affirmed.

Often the program dictates that an affirmation of the beliefs of the institution be uttered at some particular place in the transaction. The therapist's interpretation in psychotherapy could be regarded as similar. This is usually made at the end of a session.

Over-All Activities

In a structural approach, we can define an institution in behavioral terms. Rather than conceiving of it as a group of people, we view it as a system of customary transactional forms. Some of these transactions recruit and train people for the various roles of the institution, while others are held to carry out the various definitive procedures of the institution.

As I have already indicated, institutional transactions tend to be of three types. These are:

1 Actonic Task Performances: The members come together and carry out the task behaviors of the institution. They make a product in some institutions. In others, they repair or build the sites of transaction or fix the props used in a ceremony. Or they service themselves and each other.

2 Representational Performances: Members assemble and hold a representation or demonstration of the procedural rules and values of the institution. They may ritualistically repeat the beliefs to reaffirm them or teach them to children and novitiates. Or they may demonstrate the product, sell a customer, or explicate the ideational system to a skeptic or a potential donor.

3 Administrative Performances: Some members come together to oversee and plan the various activities. A session may be held to decide upon sanctions for a deviant member, or to institute correctional procedures; or plans may be drawn up to schedule the activities, change or expand the facilities, or meet an unexpected crisis.

To some extent, these various activities of an institution can be combined at a single transaction, but ordinarily some schedule of these types of meetings is in use. Various types are held simultaneously at different sites and successively at the same sites, for instance. The institution maintains a variety of physical structures and a schedule of transactions.

In some measure, the rules of conduct for an institution hold at all performances. A proper dress or uniform and a proper manner of bearing and mood may be expected of the members at all meetings or, in fact, in all parts of their lives. But often these modes vary with the kind of activity or with the role and station of the members, and similarly the members may have to think and state certain values, or symbols of these values. Whatever the practices of a given institution, all institutions have in common some system of representational cognitive behavior. This system includes some set of rules for decorum and procedure and some system of values and rationalizations.

In addition to the rules of procedure and conduct, an institution has ordinarily evolved a system of metastatements about the value of its activities. These usually consist of rationales, explanations, idealizations, and other kinds of lexical-cognitive activity. We can study the nature of these institutional statements by attending those transactions at the institution in which such matters are depicted and repeated. Then we know about the specific experiential contexts of institutionalized meanings. These are the remote contexts of the particular symbolic and representational behaviors of any other transaction.

But the institutional schedule, the transaction, the relationships, and the behavioral enactments of an institution are the immediate contexts of an institutional style of behavior or relatedness. The identification of these immediate contexts therefore allows a knowledgeable observer to know the specific meanings and connotations that obtain.

Comment: Institutionalized Styles and Meanings

The evolution of an emic system and the institutionalization of certain of its meanings have to have occurred together. In some cases, the emic meanings of a culture and the special institutional meanings are the same, or virtually the same. The Catholic and Sicilian uses of certain meanings, for example, could hardly be distinguished or attributed a separate evolution. But in other cases a particular emic meaning has been institutionalized in a variety of different institutions, so it has multiple connotations in the same society. Most institutions have altered a great many meanings by their usage. Hardly any of the experiences and meanings of a culture have escaped the value judgments of a religion, for instance. As a consequence, it is difficult to think of any meaning in English that does not have one or more special communicational uses, or at least a set of connotations that derive from some past institutional association.

It is probably safe to say that virtually all the styles and connotations we will discover in an emic system are institutionalized. Even when stylistic variations can be attributed to physical defects, illness, lifelong moods, and other non-institutional factors, their appearances have usually been attributed an institutional significance. Even when a participant uses a style and connotation unfamiliar to us, we must be careful about claiming that it is unique or idiosyncratic. It may be that we are not familiar with that institutional usage. Most of the unusual meanings we encounter have been acquired by past experience in some group or other, and even when an individual innovates a stylistic usage, it probably becomes institutionalized or else disappears from the emic system rather quickly.

By the rules of an institution, members are constrained to go to certain places at certain times, take particular roles, and carry out particular tasks. And they are to act in certain ways while they are doing these things.

The members of an institution may be required to dress a certain way, at least for formal meetings in the institution. At formal meetings of the institution, all members may wear a particular uniform or style of clothing. They may also wear a particular hairdo or type of cosmetics or at least keep these features of dress within a certain acceptable range. And they may display insignia or carry institutionally specific props.

Sometimes these features of dress are ritualistically prescribed. A bearing, manner, or mood may also be prescribed for a transaction of the institution. The members are to carry their bodies in a certain way and hold certain face sets; for example, to indicate solemnity, or rapt attention, or the like. The participants may be required to *feel* a certain mood in addition to looking that way. They must learn in such cases to develop sadness, awe, gaiety, or anger whenever they participate.

And the customs of the institution may demand that certain representational behavior be repeated at each transaction. The participants may have to say or chant or sing certain traditional units of language behavior. They may do this in unison or individually, aloud or silently. They may be required, then, to *think* certain thoughts at the transaction.

In other words, the customs of an institution prescribe how one is to think and feel as well as what one is to do at an institutional transaction. Knowing this, it is difficult to hold to the old Platonic and psychological notion that affect and thought *cause* behavior. All these activities are demanded in common by institutional prescriptions and are therefore elicited together by the contexts of an institutional event.

In some institutional transactions, however, the representational behavior of that institution may not be enacted routinely. It may, for example, appear only under certain circumstances, as when an observer or a novitiate is present. For instance, the motto of the company is not repeated every time the workmen assemble, and the transaction is not blessed if it consists only of a private meeting or a cleaning-up routine. If the representational procedure is carried out for a visitor, it may be performed by an institutional member who explains and rationalizes the enactment as he performs it. Or the representational behavior of an institution may appear only when someone forgets what he is supposed to do or when he acts uncooperatively and is adjudged to be in need of reminding.

Style

One is now in a position to define institutional style. It consists of a particular way of enacting some customary sequence of behavior. The form of the behavior will be that of some particular emic system or cultural tradition, but the manner or demeanor will be altered in a way that is characteristic for that particular institution. Thus, for example, the preacher may speak in English and wear Western clothing, but he will use a particular form of resonant and dulcet vocal qualities; he will use seventeenth-century word forms such as "thou"; and the suit he wears may be black and his collar may be worn backwards. The corporate executive, too, may speak a particular language in a repertoire of positions. But he may sit very erectly, jut his jaw, and speak quite loudly. He may wear his hair in a crew-cut style and display a small flag or a lodge pin in his lapel.

These features of behavior are associated, by convention, with particular ideas and meanings. As a consequence, when we observe any of these stylistic features, we can predict that the others will probably occur. If we see a configuration of them, we can identify a particular institutional event and tradition. Then, if we know the values and beliefs of that institution, we can predict or infer certain systems of meaning that are at least implied.

Any of the forms of an emic system can thus be used in, and varied according to the traditions of, a particular institution. I will use the term "style," then, for the variants of a behavioral form that are specific to the traditions and practices of a particular institution.

The behaviors of institutions may show certain specific styles *at all levels of integration.* Certain styles of speech and gesture, dress, and orientation are prescribed for the contributions of individual members. (These will be described in Chapter Seven.) Certain styles of relationship are used in the various transactions of the institution. The various transactions of the institution occur at particular sites and occasions and follow customary programs that prescribe and govern their tasks and progression. Finally, an institution has a schedule of different kinds of transactions to carry out its various purposes.

An institution will also make statements about the proper performance of these procedures, based on values and beliefs about their significance. Thus, emic meanings are used and valued in certain ways. These statements of meaning are repeated at certain transactions of the institution and represented at still others.

As a consequence, we can identify a particular institutional connotation by its style and by the immediate contexts in which it is represented.[2] From the standpoint of the culture at large, the immediate context specifies a particular institutional usage and connotation of an emic meaning.

[2] This statement about the relations of style and meaning could be elaborated in a variety of ways. For instance, one could affirm that people of certain appearance, character, disposition, mood, and the like are recruited for certain institutional memberships and take particular roles in these institutions that reinforce these traits. So a relation between institutional tradition, meaning, and personality can be postulated, and we can even claim that the identification of personality qualities in the style of behavior may predict a proclivity for certain uses of meaning.

Section Three

Variations: Differences Among Participants

Participants will enact customary parts in traditional programs in "their own" ways. Some differences in forms and style reflect their institutional memberships (as described in the previous chapter); others indicate emic background (Chapter Six). Still others reflect characteristics of personality or mood (Chapter Seven). These differences, too, carry connotations.

Chapter Six

Variations with Background

Some features of the forms and styles that a person has learned in his culture and institutional experience are carried over into any part he takes. We can observe these features of his behavior and identify his origins and institutional experience, and thus derive information about the meanings and values he is likely to hold.

As discussed in Section I, the form of behavior is specific to a particular cultural and subcultural tradition. Here are a few examples.

We watched a videotape of two middle-aged women having a conversation in a living room. The sound was turned off, but we could guess the ethnicity of the two women: Both were quite thin and both had long black hair tied in a knot. One was very light-complexioned, the other very dark, almost black. We could guess from the hairstyle and phenotype that the light-complexioned woman was of western Mediterranean origin and the dark woman was probably Latin American.

As we watched them move, however, we identified them both, with much more certainty, as Latin American. They acted continually in a markedly courting manner. Each of them sat erect and continually put one hand on the hip. Periodically, both turned their torsos slightly to the right and brought up their right arms so that their right hands preened the hair. In doing so, the right breast of each was presented to the other. The right palm was also presented to the reciprocal partner, and both women rolled their eyes, cocked their heads, and raised their brows and eyelids.

If one did not know something about this culture, he might misunderstand and think these women were trying to seduce one another. But their children were present, and actually they were talking about crime and politics. When we turned on the sound track, we heard that they were speaking in Spanish.

On another day, we studied several movies of men talking to a group. We noticed three men of about the same age and phenotype. All were stocky, black-haired, and dark-complexioned. We could guess that they were southern European, but could not be sure at a glance where they were from until we observed their gesticulations: The first man gesticulated actively and through a broad range of movements. His entire arms moved from the shoulders through a range of almost six by four feet. He brought them over his head on occasion and he often brought them out about a foot on each side of his body.

We could guess that he was southern Italian. He showed a trace of Italian dialect in his speech. He later told us his name was Tony and said that his parents came from Naples.

The gesticulation patterns of the second man were very different: He held his elbows at his sides and moved only the forearms and hands. These moved in an area about two feet square in front of him. He raised them as high as his face on occasion, but usually kept them at waist height. He almost never moved them laterally more than six inches beyond the sides of his body.

We can recognize this gesticulation pattern as eastern European Jewish. The difference between southern Italian and Jewish gesticulation was originally described by Efron (1941).

The third man used yet a different pattern of gestures as he spoke: He had his legs crossed, and he placed both wrists on his knees. From this position he tended to move just the hands, which were outstretched toward his auditors. On occasion, he brought one hand up in front of him in a much wider excursion, but for the most part he used a very small space for gesticulation, perhaps one foot square.

This pattern is usual for the British Isles or old English-American. However, we could have told that he was British and not British-American by the way he crossed his legs. He placed his upper knee in a position that is very uncomfortable for Americans. The upper knee was directly over the lower one, not six inches back on the thigh, in the American manner. This difference was pointed out to me by Birdwhistell in 1962.

The Lancaster dialect identified this man's background. Interpersonal spacing in the reciprocal relationship also varies with ethnicity. Certain northern European-Americans, such as the British, stand just out of tactile range in standing relationships, a distance of about four feet apart. This distance is about six inches less in eastern European Jewish culture, so the participants are within tacticle range of one another. The difference is apparently associated with the tendency for little tactile contact in British culture, at least in public, and the inverse tendency for high tactility in eastern Jewish culture. The French and certain Latin Americans we have studied use shorter interpersonal distances than the eastern European Jews. For example, Cubans often face each other less than two feet apart.

We can identify, on bases like these, the majority of subjects who are monocultural, just as we can identify them on the basis of their native language or by traces of dialect when they speak English. In fact, the kinesic and spacing patterns of European-Americans tend to persist into the second and third generations, long after these descendants have acculturated completely in dress, language, and customs.

The behaviors of an emic system appear in specific variant forms in the various enclaves and regional areas of cultural distribution. Dialects, for example, occur among English-speakers in various regions.

The most obvious example is provided by the various dialectic uses of English in regions of the United States,

Britain, South Africa, and so on. Skilled linguists in any of these countries have no difficulty identifying the region of origin of any native speaker of the language. In fact, the distinctive features of dialectic style are carefully plotted in detailed atlases of English and eastern American regions. And even the layman can identify the southern drawl, the terminal *r* of Boston, or the terminal *g* of Long Island.

There are differences in vocabulary in these various regions as well. One says "straighten up the house" in eastern Pennsylvania and "redd up" in central Pennsylvania, for example. Specific subemic variants are used in an enclave. If an immigrant learns English in such an enclave, he learns that particular system of variants.

Mrs. V. was a case in point. She used what we loosely call an Italian-American dialect. But her speech was actually specific for the southern-Italian-Americans of South Philadelphia. She did not make up a variety of substandard English on her own when she came from Italy to America. Rather, she learned a specific subcultural variant generally used in the Philadelphia enclave in which she lived.

The subemic system can identify the origins, migration pathway, and present subcultural location of its user. Similar generalizations can be made about the speech forms of various social-class categories.

Subcultural variants are also evident and distinctive in non-speech behavior. Birdwhistell (1963) is able to identify people of many of the regions of the United States by their facial sets. He points out, for instance, that the brows of people from Wisconsin and adjoining areas are characteristically smooth, because they are not used in forming facial gestures, as in other regions of the United States. There are also regional and class differences in clothing style, hairdo, and so forth.

Programs of transaction also differ by region and class. Middle-class American courtship, for example, is traditionally different from working-class dating patterns (see Chapter Four). Even the kinds of drinks that are served at a party seem to distinguish social class in America: In most parts of America, beer is served at a working-class party while shots of rye whiskey are provided for brothers or special guests in the kitchen. But the lower-middle-class drink is often a highball, and the upper-middle-class preference is for scotch, bourbon, or cocktails. Pinochle and poker are common in the working class, while bridge is played in the upper-middle class.

Eventually, we may be able to identify distinctive variants of informative behavior that are specific for a clan or a family. If so, we will then be able to identify the cultural histories of a great many characteristics that we currently define as idiosyncratic and attribute to unique personality traits. An observer's notion that a form of speech or gesture is idiosyncratic usually reflects his ignorance of other cultures and subcultures. Actually, it is highly unlikely that a variant has been invented *de novo* by an individual and is limited to his repertoire alone. Such variants are non-communicative unless their use spreads.

Such innovations of form and meaning do occur in institutions. These may become generally adopted in that institution and then spread widely across ethnic and regional lines. We can assume that such a process has occurred over and over in the history of man.

Variations of form and meaning occur, according to institutional membership and role within a cultural category. Furthermore, since men and women of various age groups do not use the same portions of the emic repertoire of their culture, all members of a culture do not use the same repertoire of emic forms and meanings. (The reader will notice that I have avoided using the term "style" for these variations. I have reserved this term to designate variations in institutional usage, discussed in the previous chapter.)

Word choice, gesture, and paralinguistic qualities vary with culture and subculture; so do forms of dress and décor. Specific variations in behavioral form also occur at higher levels of behavioral integration. Interpersonal distance, the configurations of address and relationship, and the programs for assembling a depiction also vary in specific ways with culture and subculture. Furthermore, the objects, ecological events, and experiences of different peoples are not the same. As a consequence, there may not be equivalent contextual experiences across cultural lines, and meanings may not be the same.

We must remember, then, that variants of form are not usually isolated occurrences. They occur together in the repertoire of a person. If we see a person employ a specific kind of word usage, inflectional pattern, dress, or relational form, we can predict that he knows and will use the others of an emic or subemic system. If he does not, we must assume that he is not native to that system. If he does, we can identify his origins and predict the system of meanings he is using. The forms of behavior that a person or a group of people employ designate a specific contextual reference or meaning, and the *type* of forms they use identifies a system of emic meanings.

If one is participating in a transaction within his own culture, the traditional forms he uses are consonant with the expectations of the others. But he may travel or migrate and join a group that uses a different emic system. In this case, the forms and meanings he uses will be non-consonant, to some degree, with the definition of the current situation.

At one extreme, this non-consonance may be so great that he cannot act meaningfully in the transaction. In other cases, special provisions are made for his foreign experience so that he can engage, but misunderstandings are likely. To some degree, the foreigner may learn the forms and meanings of the emic system of his new group, but he will probably retain behavioral features of his background that are recognizable and identifiable. We can also guess that the traditional meanings and values of his earlier background are carried over, and that these at least influence his participation and his interpretations of the newer experience.

Members of an institution take the styles of that institution wherever they go. In this way, institutional styles are carried over to other roles and activities. When such institutional styles are identified out of the institutional context, they provide information from which a knowledgeable observer can make certain inferences about the performer's meanings.

Customary institutional styles may thus appear in transactions outside the institution. A person who has status in an institution or membership in a prestigious institution, for example, may display the insignia, uniforms, props, symbolic words, or styles of bearing of that institution wherever he goes. The young physician, for instance, may carry his stethoscope everywhere and show his professional demeanor as he talks to the guests at a party.

Members of a total institution may learn the stylistic features of an institutional program so thoroughly that they cannot take part in any transactions without showing these characteristics. In such cases, we can usually predict that they will impute particular connotations to the representation of at least certain meanings.

Some people are so involved in affiliation to certain institutions that they carry out the enactments of that institution even when these are inappropriate to the immediate context. A religious zealot may preach and proselytize at *all* meetings, and the young psychotherapist may take to listening and making interpretations about everyone's behavior. Family roles may also be carried over to all transactions. Some people thus take a motherly role in all performances, and others may relate to them in the reciprocal role of child.

This is a major factor in deviance. The roles that we designate as deviant are often institutionalized to begin with, and many members of a deviant institution rather compulsively re-enact these performances in a variety of contexts. Sometimes they seem to do so exhibitionistically, but it may be that the performances are unwittingly expected of them by partners outside the institution or even by the society at large (Erikson, 1966). In any event, we have characteristic behavioral styles and performances that psychiatrists can label "alcoholic," "schizophrenic," "psychopathic," "hysterical," "homosexual," and so on.

A variety of factors may enhance the tendency to carry

over qualities of an institutional performance. The institutional features may be so widespread in common culture that they have become general qualities of an emic performance. As a consequence, these are used generally in a culture. Or the institution may be total (Goffman, 1961A) and demand of its members that all of their behavior shows adherence to the styles and beliefs of the institution. Many people use the styles and emblems of an institution only when they are within the institution, or else they use these outside only to affirm or indicate an institutional membership when they meet a fellow member. But people who gain status by holding a role in a prestigious institution may displace its styles to all occasions. And zealots may exaggerate institutional styles and repeat institutional clichés ad nauseam.

In cases in which an individual is strongly affiliated with an institution, the styles of that institution may pervade everything he does. His behavior is overridingly involved with the practices of that institution, and his thoughts and meanings clearly reflect that system of beliefs and values. In fact, we may not see evidences in his behavior of other institutional memberships.

But most people belong to a variety of institutions, or at least they have held multiple memberships at various times in their lives. In such a case, an individual may show a variety of styles. Some of these may appear in certain relationships or situations, and other styles may appear on other occasions; or an individual may show mixtures of institutional styles in a single performance. In such cases (if we have enough sophistication about institutions), we may be able to reconstruct the memberships he has held. But we will have to be careful about guessing what institutional meanings govern his interpretations of an experience.

People who have grown up in a single emic and subemic tradition and learned to behave in a single influential institution may have very simple, homogeneous repertoires of behavioral forms and styles. But cosmopolitans may have lived in several emic, subemic, and institutional traditions.

Such people may have the ability to participate in multiple transactions with high comprehension about what is going on and with incredible adaptive skill for mustering the appropriate segments of their repertoire.

In the case of people who have multiple behavioral styles and experience with many subsystems of meaning, we must be very careful about guessing which meaning they may be using at a given time. But we should not turn away, on this account, from the attempt to make systematic inferences about meaning. As I will describe in later chapters, people who have mixed repertoires of styles and meanings ordinarily indicate which of a set of meanings they are employing by their metacommunicative activity. They accentuate or exhibit a particular style, for instance, or provide us with an identifying kinesic signal.

I am implying here a rather extravagant claim, which I would like to make explicit. I hold that we can use stylistic differences to systematically identify and predict the cognitive values and meanings that govern a member's actions, if we take the trouble to be careful observers of stylistic features.

In the past, we have lacked sufficient data to do so, but we have also shied away from generalizations like this. We tend to deny pattern. We are addicted to romantic notions about the spontaneity and originality of our actions, and we exaggerate differences between individuals. We like to parrot truisms such as "I am an individual."

These cherished Western notions about individuality can be supported by the careful misuse and misinterpretation of psychological research. We can stick strictly to subjects within our own ethnic, class, and institutional backgrounds. Since the forms are the same in such a sample, we can focus on differences in the styles of individuals and attribute these to idiosyncratic experiences, genetic differences, and the like. We thus systematically avoid learning about other cultures and other institutions, so we do not see differences that are incidental to tradition. In fact, we classify any differences incident to culture as deviancies or corruptions in learning. Black English, for instance, is considered a pidgin form of standard English, spoken by those who did not or cannot learn to speak properly.

If one systematically denies the commonalities of behavior in a culture or an institution and stays within his own cultural and social groups, he will not meet many people of different backgrounds. He can thus consider the behavioral features of the few people he meets from these outside groups to be idiosyncratic. Thus, if one knows one Syrian, he may call that fellow's behaviors idiosyncratic, provided he does not visit Syria and discover the systematic similarities of that culture.

The belief in individuality can be maintained by another conceptual trick. To be sure, the *total* repertoires of cosmopolitans are widely divergent. But among those of the same institutional background, certain specific features will be highly similar. The similarities can be denied by pointing to the differences that accumulate in the total experiences of two people.

But I think the main difference between a view of patterned similarities, as is developing in communication theory, and a view of individual differences, as emerges in the psychodynamic sciences, arises from the fact that the two sciences concentrate on different data. The structuralist who studies communication examines patterns of motor behavior by direct observation. He emphasizes the congruence of these to explain communication. But the psychodynamicist examines cognitive experience by subjectivist methods. He thus uncovers separate interpretations of the beliefs and myths of institutional systems and the integrations of many of these that an individual has tried to make. These myths emphasize divergence and individuality, for it is characteristic of Western myth systems to allow a belief in individuality and spontaneity within an institution; it is equally characteristic of Western institutions as a whole to foster the belief that they are special and unique.

Chapter Seven

"Individual" Variations

The members of a single cultural and institutional tradition vary in their performances of the same type of transaction. They show styles and preferences which indicate meanings that are not simply institutional.

The Transcontextual Performance

If an acculturated member of a tradition is attending a transaction with which he has had experience, he knows his part in the activity and he knows what behavior is expected of him at each spot in the program. If he performs at a certain spot some wholly other action, his performance is "non-programmatic" by the definition I have given. But when this enactment is a recognizable unit of activity—a unit that ordinarily belongs to some other situation—his performance is called "transcontextual" (Bateson, 1972). We assume that he has some other context and some other program of action in mind. Apparently he has behaved in accordance with his own cognitive context instead of complying with the programming of the situation as it has been defined.

Marge often did this in the psychotherapy session. Although the situation had been defined as a formal narrative and psychotherapy session, she kept exhibiting her legs. She made sexual and provocative statements such as, "I want to be raped," and she called the physician "Bud."

The transcontextual performance may occur at any level of integration. The non-programmatic act may be as small as the addition of an extra "eh" or "uh" to the syntactic sentence or the breakthrough of a sob or a sigh. Or an uncustomary utterance may be made. The entire participation can also be transcontextual. One may take a role usually reserved for someone of another age group or gender, or he may perform doggedly the behaviors expected at another transaction or in other institutions. I remember once attending the wrong cocktail party. Neither I nor anyone else, as far as I could tell, noticed the incongruence until more than an hour after I had arrived.

When a person acts transcontextually, we say he is not paying attention, or else that he is unable or unwilling to do his part. Often we can recognize a non-programmatic unit of behavior and identify the programs of activity to which it usually belongs. In everyday life we might say that the participant is acting like a baby or an old woman or a hoodlum, and various metastatements of value may be placed on this performance.

The psychological sciences would make an inference of motivation in such cases. We would assume that the participant wants to carry out the program of activity from which his transcontextual action has been borrowed. We would accordingly locate this inference in some theoretical class of motivations or drives. We might, for example, say that he is motivated by sexual or hostile wishes.

If a person repeatedly and characteristically carries out an enactment that results in attacks or scolding by others, we would say he is self-defeating or masochistic. If he repeatedly fails to perform active parts, we may say he is passive, and so forth.

In psychodynamic approaches, we also try to explain persistent non-programmatic performances. Freud attributes them to psychic determinism (S. Freud, 1959). This pattern, acquired in childhood, is compulsively repeated in many contexts. In psychoanalytic theory, the subject does this because he unconsciously imagines he is still acting in the contexts of his childhood. Psychoanalysts would call such transcontextual acting "transference." When the non-progammatic behavior occurs among children or resembles the behavior of children, the analyst would term it "regressive" and attribute it a given phase of infancy according to the psychoanalytic schema of psychosexual development.

Sometimes the non-programmatic performance is explained as a defensive reaction on the part of the performer. This inference is based on the observation or inference that certain events in the actual context are perceived as threatening in some way. To be sure, some non-programmatic performances seem to obscure or conceal other behavior the participant is enacting.

In a behavioral systems view, we would not make psychological inferences until we had carried out a prior operation. We would collect a series of episodes in which a given non-programmatic behavior occurred, and then we would search the contexts of each one in the hope of finding certain visible and audible occurrences that *each time* accompanied the variation in question. Then we would explain the variation by describing the contextual situation with which it was interdependent.

Non-programmatic Features of the Enactment

It may be that a proper performance is contributed to a customary transaction, but the performance may only have certain qualities or features that are not usual or appropriate.

Collectively, the non-language sounds and the vocal qualifiers have been termed paralanguage (Trager, 1958). In linguistics, these dimensions of speech behavior are distinguished from the structural features and content. Characteristic vocal qualifiers are raspiness, nasality, overloudness or oversoftness, overfastness or overslowness, clippedness, and drawl.

Mrs. V. tended to speak oversoftly and flatly or blandly—using few variations of vocal qualifiers. The psychiatrists abstracted expressive and schizophrenic qualities from Mrs. V.'s speech (see below). Marge, on the other hand, showed a wide range of paralinguistic qualities. She would mumble inaudibly one minute and be overloud the next. She changed her rate of speech from overslow to overfast. She sometimes spoke in a singsong rhythm. Psychiatrists judged

Marge's speech to be highly affective, or emotional, and used these qualities as one basis for diagnosing her "schizo-affective schizophrenia" (see Chapter Ten).

Vocal qualifiers have been of special interest to psychological scientists, since they provide indicators of mood or affect (Gottschalk, 1961; Eldred and Price, 1958; Pittenger, Hockett, and Danehy, 1960).

We should bear in mind, however, that certain patterns of vocal qualifiers are also indicative of dialect, class, and ethnicity. Drawl occurs throughout the southern United States, and oversoftness is highly valued by middle-class Americans (Trager and Smith, 1956).

Word choice also varies with region of the country, social class, and other categorical memberships. The women spoke of "mind pictures," for example. Word choice and pronunciations, together with favored paralinguistic qualities, occur together as typical dialectical patterns. Marge and Mrs. V. used a clearly recognizable dialectical pattern typical of the large Southern-Italian-American enclave in South Philadelphia.

As in the case of language, posture and movement can have a variety of qualities. One can move languidly or jerkily, in small or grand excursion, and so forth. Accordingly we are justified in speaking of kinesic and postural styles or of parakinesic qualities (Birdwhistell, 1969). As in the case of paralanguage, these features may characterize a dialectal area or institution, and are not necessarily a non-programmatic feature of one individual's behavior.[1]

A parakinesic quality may pervade all of the behavior of a participant. The parakinesic qualities of Mrs. V. and Marge paralleled their paralinguistic traits. Mrs. V. was underactive to the point of moving depressively. Her lack

[1] As is also the case with paralanguage, kinesic signals have been viewed in psychology and psychiatry as expressions of idiosyncratic states or personality (Mahl, 1966; Berger, 1958; Ekman, 1967; Gottschalk, 1961). There is no reason to doubt that the *styles* of performing these signals, and perhaps the number of signals deemed necessary, reflect personality qualities. But one must also recognize their cultural regularity and see their significance for identifying regions. *They are only idiosyncratic if they are not usual in some cultural category.*

of movement was especially noteworthy in view of her Italian background, for members of this culture ordinarily move often and in a wide range of arm and hand excursion.

Marge was generally overactive. She sat up, sprawled, stood, crossed and uncrossed her legs, and so forth. She also moved rapidly and broadly, throwing her arms and body around in wide excursion. Although much movement is abnormal to a degree for an adult, it did show the mobility of Italian-American kinesics more typically than did Mrs. V.'s behavior.

We can explain Mrs. V.'s dialect on the basis of her origins in Sicilian-American culture. She also spoke about "ice" (Italian water ice) and street carnivals (an enclave custom in Italian-American parts of South Philadelphia). So her behavior was replete with indications of her regional and ethnic origins. But Mrs. V.'s immobility cannot be explained on these bases.

Marge also showed Italian-American and South Philadelphia dialectical styles, but she was markedly overactive in her behavior at times. She exhibited herself and flopped about on the sofa. This behavior is neither regional nor ethnic. The psychiatrist would point out that the relative absence of gesticulation, facial movement, and changing voice qualities made up a picture of "flattened affect," which is said to be an indication of schizophrenia. And, conversely, the overactivity of Marge—the continual gesturing and movement—were indications of the schizoaffective type of schizophrenia. So were Marge's inappropriate utterances and sexy exposures.

So we can distinguish the usual qualities of an emic tradition from behaviors that are inappropriate to that emic tradition. But the matter is not simple. Schizoaffective schizophrenia is said to be more common in southern Italians, for instance, than among other groups.

Also, Marge varied her demeanor and parakinesic styles with the position she used. When she was sitting with her mother, she was slow, dissociative, and non-courting in style. Later, when she was contending, her face and body were animated. She showed a range of styles. Her body came into the hypertonus of the courtship state. She was alert, overfast, and widely excursive in her range of movement. Her demeanor changed kaleidoscopically, with facial expressions of anger, depression, dominance, humor, and so forth. Marge also used characteristically Italian gestures during the sessions when she sat with her mother.

I would make the following guess. Marge had learned two paralinguistic and parakinesic styles: one she used in her family, at least when relating to her mother, and the other she used in relationships with people outside the family, maybe with men. Possibly she had learned the second from her father, from some other relatives, or from peers in her neighborhood.

Systematic studies of movement style in schizophrenic subjects have been made by Davis (1970). But we cannot be content to put people in the diagnostic categories of psychiatry if we are to understand their behavior in general and their stylistic variants in particular.

Marge showed styles of behavior that we ordinarily associate with anger. She protruded her jaw, she made direct face-to-face confrontations to Mrs. V., and she raised her voice. But these were transient and related to immediate contexts of the sessions. We would not say she was an angry person. The same thing can be said about her tendency to fall into slow movement and the facial set of depression.

But all people show behaviors like this, which we attribute to certain moods or feeling states. Some participants smile often, appear active, move with bounce, and otherwise indicate states we call happy. Others sit with sagging face and move slowly and thus suggest a depressive mood. It is worthwhile to distinguish between temporary and permanent displays of such indicators. Thus, Marge's depressive appearance was intermittent, while Mrs. V.'s depressive quality lasted throughout the session. We might say that Marge indicated phases of depression, but that Mrs. V. was depressed.

In such cases, the affective indicators did not appear to

vary with the vicissitudes of the transaction, so they suggested a more persistent state, related to the larger contexts of her life situation.

There are, of course, a great many other features of demeanor and bearing that can be used to make further inferences about the personality traits or affective states of a participant, but these matters have been detailed in the psychological literature (Mahl, 1966; Ekman, 1965, 1967; Exline and Winters, 1965; Berger, 1958). Despite the existence of a large number of ideas about the expressions of intrapsychic and organismic states, I will not personally find such research acceptable until workers have taken the cultural and institutional dimensions of behavior into account. Only when expected forms of behavior and demeanor for a culture, subculture, and institution have been identified can we speak systematically of deviations and idiosyncratic qualities. Such research can be done by observing multiple performances of customary transactions in various cultures and institutions. So far, no one has done this in detail.

In addition, a person may indicate illness by pallor, flushed cheeks, weakness and tremor, coughing, wheezing, inattentiveness, wincing, and a variety of other behaviors and parakinesic styles.

I will use the term "paracommunicative" to refer to the performance styles and qualities of any unit of behavior (see Comment, p. 117).

In the past, instead, we have tended to do in research what people do in everyday life. We have tended to impute our own cultural and institutional values to behavior, as I will now describe.

Emic and Institutional Connotations

Institutions have a tendency to value and impute meanings to behaviors and deportments that they do not prescribe. Meanings are ascribed to deviant performances and to alien behaviors, for instance. And certain moods and states of health are given meaning and handled in certain ways within the institution. Styles of behavior that are not part of an institution may still have meaning within that institution. As a consequence, members of an institution have institutionalized reactions to the perception of certain forms and styles of behavior.

A style of behavior can be influenced by organismic states that are not simply learned in an institution or culture. Mood, for instance, can be a necessary feature of institutional behavior, and its persistent carry-over may result in a permanent, learned mood. But other factors may also determine mood, and other organismic states may influence the style of behavior. For example, certain phenotypical characteristics of individuals will affect their ability to perform and may also influence the relations others form with them. The same thing can be said about physical disabilities and chronic illnesses. In fact, the appearance of unusual organismic qualities in childhood may profoundly influence the cultural experience of an individual.

Health may also influence performance. There are, of course, a series of indicators of health, and a display of these is often made at the beginning of a transaction to indicate the capacities of a participant and elicit certain allowances for the performance.

These states certainly influence behavioral performance and may even result in particular styles of performance. In fact, they are sometimes used as a basis for the identification and diagnosis of illness, and they are often simplistically attributed to genetic transmission or infantile experience and used as the basis for personality typing. But the appearance of these traits in an individual may lead him into certain institutional roles even in childhood, through which he may end up as a member of a total institution. In this way, these traits are often maintained and shaped by institutional procedures.

But an institution may have evolved certain ideas about these states. It may carry theories about their nature and origin, their value, and their permissibility. The members of an institution may experience certain meanings any time they observe the signs of such organismic states.

Furthermore, an institution may prescribe that certain

courses are to be taken on behalf of people in certain states. It may be considered necessary to avoid them or make special allowances for them. Sometimes, special procedures are prescribed for the management of these people so that they may be indoctrinated in particular roles or even taken into custody in special institutions where they are treated or sometimes further trained into the roles of mystic, patient, and so on.

Special institutional arrangements have evolved in many traditions for the confinement and maintenance of deviants such as the handicapped, dependent children, religious recluses, professional soldiers, and sometimes aliens. Often these institutions are total, in Goffman's terms (1961A). They demand exclusive memberships and prescribe all aspects of a member's activity and belief. In other cases, they provide special economic supports, special work roles, and special allowances for participation in social groups.

The institutionalization of schizophrenia is a case in point. It is not known whether the difficulties of schizophrenic people are congenital or are developed in early childhood. In either event, these individuals usually hold special roles in the family. These roles may maintain or even cause them to behave in special, deviant ways. The behavioral programs and styles that these people use are typical and patterned. They are sufficiently similar from case to case to allow them to be considered as "illnesses" which have "diagnostic signs."

When a schizophrenic person is separated from his complementary partner, he often becomes unable to function. He is then institutionalized in a mental hospital. Here he is indoctrinated to accept certain kinds of dependent relationships and roles and carry out the routine behaviors of hospital life. He is also given a diagnostic category that carries certain implications in the social system of meanings.

Other kinds of deviants may be specially related to close partners who at one and the same time control and unwittingly maintain the deviance. The subjects learn stylized performances and special myth systems from other deviants of the same type. Eventually such people may end up in institutions such as prisons or mental hospitals.

The final outcome of such channels of development and learning is a specific institutional set of styles and meanings held in common by types of deviants. The behavior of alcoholics, schizophrenics, prostitutes, and homosexuals, for example, is recognizable at a glance in such an in-group and is used as the basis for diagnostic typing in the social system as a whole. These behavioral variants are the subject of institutionalized theories, value judgments, and policies of management in other institutions of a society.

Institutionalized meanings may be applied to the behaviors of a foreigner. The institution may have evolved a set of stereotypes and values about foreigners in general or about people of specific ethnic groups and institutions. In this case, the observation of an emic form or institutional style in the behavior of an outsider may trigger a set of inferences and judgments that influence or govern what happens next.

These behaviors are not a subject of conscious concern; communication can be a highly efficient process under certain conditions. It would be impossible to deal with these thousands of microacts' in cognition and still attend to the more conscious necessities of interpretation, tactics, and decision-making. However, the failure to know about these matters and the tendency for mythical explanation does make for a great deal of miscommunication among deviant performers and those of different cultural backgrounds. In the case of cross-cultural communication, for instance, there is a marked tendency to misidentify the origins of other people, to hold to stereotypes concerning them, and to maintain automatic prejudice.

Comment: Paracommunication

Changes in the qualities of voicing have been classified as one dimension of paralanguage (Trager and Smith, 1956). These styles of voice quality often reflect subemic variation. Drawl, it has been noted, is characteristic of speech in the southern United States. Institutional styles may also be reflected in vocal modifiers. The dulcet tones of preaching are an example. These vocal qualities, like facial displays, are often attributed to organismic states such as mood (Pittenger, Hockett, and Danehy, 1960; Pittenger and Smith, 1957).

Analogously, Birdwhistell (1969) has called the qualities of body movement "parakinesic." Variations in the excursion and speed of gesturing, for instance, and the use of qualities such as gracefulness or awkwardness are presumed to provide metacommunicative qualifications analogous to those of paralinguistic variants. Collectively, I will call these qualities of style "paracommunicative."

Hence the process of inferring background and cognitive meanings can be called "paracommunicative inference." Researchers use such inference in determining the cultural and institutional memberships of a subject, and psychologists use them to make inferences about personality type and affective state. But the participants of a transaction in everyday life also make such inferences about their fellow participants.

If a participant moves in a French style because he was born and reared in that country, we would hardly claim that he is using this style on purpose in order to show us that he is French. The inference we might make about his origins, as well as the deductions we would make about him in general, constitute a paracommunicative inference.

If, however, he tells us that he *is* French, or if he wears some insignia to demonstrate this fact, we can say that he is *behaving* paracommunicatively. On this basis, all the behavior of wearing uniforms or insignia or otherwise *displaying* ethnicity, class, institutional memberships, or organismic states will be termed paracommunicative behavior.[1]

If we can observe that the interactional behavior of a transaction is dependent upon paracommunicative behaviors, or paracommunicative inference, we can speak of paracommunication. Thus, a person may respond with hostility to a foreign accent and thus escalate a cross-cultural difficulty; or a person who indicates depression may elicit special responses from others, and these events may influence the subsequent events and styles of that transactional performance.

In short, then, qualities of behaving provide a vast system of information about the people who are taking part. So complicated is this body of information that it may pay us to order it by levels, using a schema something as follows:

Paracommunicative features at level 1 tell us something about the health, personality, and social position of a participant. This sort of information may determine the particular enactments, parts, and roles that each person takes or is awarded at any given transaction. It may also determine the kinds of transactions that he will attend or be invited to attend.

---

[1] I do not want to attempt any hard and fast distinction between paracommunicative inference and paracommunicative behavior; I do not know enough about the behaviors in question, and the matter seems relative. We would hardly say that a recent Italian immigrant was speaking Italian in order to communicate "Italianness." We would infer his Italian origins from his speech, but not jump to a teleological explanation. However, there are situations in which the issue would be quite in doubt. If an Italian-American politician, for instance, who spoke English well, were to speak Italian, we might well say that he is doing so to indicate "Italianness."

Paracommunicative features at level 2 will tell us about the established relationships of a person. Social commitments among persons who know each other may determine the involvements and alliances in a transaction and the attendance of certain subgroups in a schedule or set of transactions.

Paracommunicative features at level 3 indicate institutional affiliations and thereby indicate which kinds of transaction a person or a subgroup will attend and which loyalties, representations, values, and beliefs they are likely to maintain.

Paracommunicative features at level 4 will indicate the regional, class, and ethnic origins of participants. These features, too, determine participation of people in various activities and the status they will hold. These features also determine their forms of behaving and the values they will uphold in any given transaction.

Paracommunicative features at level 5 indicate the epistemological systems or world views of a people. We will elaborate on this issue in the last section of this volume.

We should notice that there are two ways to look at paracommunicative features. In one instance, we can concentrate on what these tell us about the characteristics of a person, a relationship, an institution, or a culture. In another view, we can concern ourselves with what difference styles and manners of performance make in the shape of an ongoing program of communicational activity.

By taking this second point of view, we observe that in some cases the differences among people and relationships make almost no observable difference in the proceedings of a communicational event. Allowances are made for the personality traits, health, memberships, and backgrounds of the participants, and the members attend primarily to the business at hand and relegate their special traits and affiliations to a secondary role. But in either case, primary attention is devoted to who people are and what they are like. Participants emphasize differences in their skill, health, mood, status, or origins. They demand special consideration on such a basis or retire from active involvement on such grounds. And the transaction may thus come to center on the traits and origins of the participants rather than on the customary program of activity. In fact, disruptive activities on a basis of personality type, class, or ethnicity, and biases about such characteristics, may keep people away altogether. They may break up an ongoing transaction or divide an entire social network or neighborhood. In such cases, we could say that the communicational processes themselves are of a paracommunicational nature.

Section Four

On Meta-communicational Behavior and Meaning

In Section I, it was claimed that all people have a repertoire of customary patterns of behavior. Some of these are employed in carrying out physical tasks and others in representing ideas or experiences. We spoke especially of the example of speech and gesture. Thus, a performance of one of these patterns of behavior designates a referent or denotes something. And when anyone performs such a pattern of behavior, other people who are familiar with it can join in performing it and/or they can assign a cognitive meaning to what they have observed.

In Section II, however, we pointed out that these enactments are performed in particular situations. So the participants frame their relationships by the use of furniture, posture, orientation, and distancing, and then they follow some customary program or agenda in putting their enactments together. These kinds of programs range from simple dyadic ones, which are used by relatives or friends to greet, court, or service each other, to more complex institutional transactions. These situational contexts specify certain connotations and thus define the meaning of any interactions or enactments that occur within them.

In Section III, we dealt with differences in enacting a pattern of behavior or a transaction—differences that were related to the characteristics of a participant, a relationship, an institution, or a culture. We held that these differences could tell us about the participant and make a difference in the events that occurred among people. Accordingly these paracommunicative features also carry connotations that further qualify the meaning of any action or interaction.

In all these instances, however, we were dealing with customary or traditional forms of audible and visible behavior which are inevitably built into the concerted performances of routine activities. In order to behave communicationally, the participants must follow a pattern and an agenda in a situation and must in the process indicate their traits, affiliations, and backgrounds. One can behave non-traditionally, but he cannot behave in a random way. He cannot behave in a vacuum or in ways other than those he has learned, and he cannot behave in ways that are not specific for his species. So participants will generally follow the governing procedures of species, culture, institution, and situation.

But people can introduce additional behavior into the customary agenda of their enactments and programs of enactment. They can add statements or gestures to their parts in a discourse and thus specify a particular connotation— or they can qualify and modify the implications of what they are saying. We will deal with some instances of this kind in Chapter Eight. Gesture and innuendo can also be used to imply or call attention to complex systems of ideation and value, as I will illustrate in Chapter Nine. And behavioral patterns can be introduced that manipulate the course of events or command a particular outcome (Chapter Ten). In fact, whole programs have evolved for changing the behavior of other people or altering a situation. The program of the psychotherapy session is an example that I will describe in Chapter Eleven.

Collectively, it is now commonplace to describe this order of communicational behavior by using the term "metacommunication," which refers to *communication about or in regard to communicational activities.*

Chapter Eight

Meta-Acts

In the course of assembling a representation, one may wittingly or unwittingly qualify or change his meaning by adding a variety of metacommunicative behaviors.[1] He can do this in a number of ways, of which I will describe and illustrate four: (1) changes in the marking behavior; (2) the intercalation of lexical units; (3) the addition of metacommunicative gestures and facial displays; and (4) changes in style and emic reference.

One "metacommunicates" about his own representational behavior. But the metacommunicative supplement can be carried out by some other group member. One group member speaks, for example; then another person comments about what the first man has said, or makes a gesture or facial display about it. Metacommunicational exchanges like these can be simple, as in this example, or of the greatest complexity.

[1] In 1955, Bateson suggested that animals must have special signals that allow them to discriminate between activities that are morphologically similar. For instance, Bateson said, two dogs may approach each other and join in play or else they may fight. There must be a metasignal, he reasoned, that they can exchange to indicate which of these similar activities is intended (Bateson, 1955). Since then, several ethologists have described such behavior (Kaufman and Rosenblum, 1966; Devore, 1965).

I see no reason why Bateson's concept of metacommunicational behavior should not be widely extended to describe any kind of behavior that qualifies, modifies, or in any way alters the stream of ongoing communicational events. Thus, verbal comments, certain gestures, and changes in marking behavior and style that modify or instruct about speech and relations—all of these can be considered metacommunicative.

Metacommunicative Changes in the Marking Behavior

The marking behavior of speech can be changed or manipulated at all levels of integration, from the contours of pitch and stress to the configurations and orientation of the total posture. A speaker can vary his pitch, stress, or marking behavior, and thereby alter the meaning of a syntactic sentence. In the Whitaker-Malone sessions, for instance, Marge sometimes addressed her mother in the lexical forms of a question, but her suprasegmental intonational manipulation pattern indicated, rather, that she was making an accusation (Scheflen, 1970):

Was I baptized?
Did I cry?
Did I get scared?

With the primary stress and pitch rise on the first morpheme, and a pitch fall on the last.

Malone also used an unusual stress and pitch pattern on occasion:

How long *can* you
    remember?
Did you *warm* the milk?
Like a *baby,* wasn't it?
Where *is* your husband?

With a primary stress and pitch rise on the underlined morph and also a pitch fall on the terminal.

The last of these syntactic sentences was especially interesting. As we noted previously, Malone addressed it to Mrs. V. at a time in the interview when no one had yet mentioned Mrs. V.'s husband. But the form he used—placing the primary stress on "is"—would ordinarily be used in a context in which the husband was already being discussed. One would have to know psychodynamic theory and the tactics of certain psychotherapists to understand this unusual form. The fact is that Marge had been speaking about being sexy in a context that could have referred to her father unconsciously. I think Malone took the reference that way and used the unusual suprasegmental pattern to make this implication. Thus he added an innuendo, a kind of metacommunicative implication, to his apparent question. This appears to be a tactical manipulation of stress and pitch of the kind we ordinarily call innuendo.

A speaker can change the lexical reference of a syntactic sentence itself by the way he uses pitch and stress. Here is a rather humorous example that Birdwhistell once described (1963).

A young psychiatrist had been treating a patient who was hospitalized for rather flagrant, antisocial homosexuality. At a point when the patient seemed improved, his psychiatrist allowed him to try a weekend leave outside the hospital.

The following Monday morning, the patient returned for his interview. We can guess that the psychiatrist had some anxiety about how his patient had behaved that weekend. His first question to the patient was: "How was your weekend?"

But the young physician used a most unusual suprasegmental pattern. He placed a primary stress on "end" instead of "week," he used a pitch fall with "week" and a pitch rise with "end," and he used a stop between "week" and "end." He thus referred to a part of his patient's anatomy, which he qualified with a descriptive adjective.

A speaker can also produce what seems like a deliberate ambiguity in the lexical reference. A hospitalized patient was visited by the chief psychiatrist, to whom he addressed the following question: "Will you be my head doctor?" In this case, the suprasegmental contours were such that it was impossible to say whether the patient used a double bar or a single bar between "head" and "doctor," and his pitch-and-stress contour was flat throughout the utterance. He thus created an ambiguity as to whether he meant doctor of his head or doctor in charge.

Sometimes the markers of the point-unit are exaggerated. The terminal kinesic act that accompanies the double-bar juncture of the declarative may be made very forcefully. Instead of bringing down the hand in a slight excursion, for instance, a fist may be banged against the other palm or against a desk.

At the end of a point-unit, the speaker may turn his face away from an auditor and thus indicate the completion of that address. Sometimes he greatly exaggerates this turning, so that his head is brought far away from the others. Whitaker sometimes did this when he finished speaking to Marge and turned to address Mrs. V. Figure 8-1 shows this.

FIGURE 8-1.   Whitaker (at right), after bringing his head far to the right and thus breaking face-to-face contact with Marge.

Since the girl was always interrupting her mother and bidding for Whitaker's attention, I presume that this exaggerated terminal was intended to break off the address with finality and discourage Marge from further attempts at a tête-à-tête. But Whitaker had just addressed a question to Marge, so one can speculate that he did not expect an answer. His question may have been rhetorical.

Sometimes the marking behavior of a speaker seems to direct others not to comment or not to answer a question about what he has just said. Such a direction may consist of staring at someone who seems about to comment. A listener may look down or away with a deadpan expression when his complementary partner speaks. Behavior such as this seems to cast doubt on the credulity of a statement.

Sometimes the marking behavior seems to be used in such a way that the referent of a remark is ambiguous or confused. A person may look down at the floor, for instance, and use an impersonal pronoun such as "someone" when he is making an unfavorable comment about another participant who is present. On the other hand, a speaker may make what seems lexically to be an impersonal remark but address the point-unit in a direct eye-to-eye confrontation to someone else at the gathering.[2]

I could give a number of other illustrations of altering the marking behavior as a way of metacommenting, but it is misleading to do so out of context. Ordinarily an utterance and/or a gesture is added to such changes, so we should talk first about these additions, so that *configurations* of metacommunicative behavior can be visualized.

Metacommunicative Speech

Communicative behavior can also be qualified by adding or intercalating metacommunicative points, positions, or even transactions. There are a variety of allomorphs for most words and phrases. These, of course, are called synonyms. Each of a set of synonyms has a similar denotative reference, so any of the set could be used in specifying a context. But synonyms are not exactly equivalent. They may have varied connotations. Some word choices, for instance, might be considered masculine, hostile, histrionic, pedantic, etc. Other synonyms convey different qualities of a contextual experience. For one reason or another, a

[2] Birdwhistell (1963) has described three types of address which he calls "modes of communicating." These are:

In "intrapersonal modes," the performer holds his head and eyes down, underprojects his voice, and converges short of his listeners—usually a few feet before himself and in the direction of the floor. He is likely in this mode to slouch, to cross his legs, and to clutch his own hands or arms. He may also feel or stroke himself or play with an object.

In the intrapersonal mode, or the mode of direct address, the participant holds his head up and looks at his vis-à-vis. He projects his voice and converges his eyes appropriately for the interpersonal distance.

In the extrapersonal mode, the speaker may hold his head up, looking above or beyond his vis-à-vis and projecting his voice beyond them. Normally this mode can be used to enlist the attention of someone outside the immediate circle of interaction, but some speakers use it to direct general remarks and some people use it habitually.

speaker may qualify his denotative reference by varying the allomorphs he adds to the sentence.

In cases in which these additions and choice may imply or suggest a meaning other than that which is denoted, we can regard them as metacommunicative. The syntactic utterance can also be qualified by paralinguistic behavior, but this matter will concern us later.

In some cases, the metacommunicative elements of the syntactic sentence are not lexical elements, but paralinguistic sounds. Sobbing, sighing, laughter, and snickering are examples. These sounds may have obvious metacommunicative reference to the veracity or literality of the syntactic utterances they accompany. But I suspect there is more to the matter. Laughter, for instance, sometimes seems to change the value or significance of an entire narrative or even of a relationship and transaction. These paralinguistic qualifiers may be metacommunicative to complex structures, as is the wink or the bowl gesture I will describe in Chapter Nine.

If the entire syntactic sentence is a comment or a qualifying statement, however, it will be a communicative unit at least as complex as a point, because the marking behavior of a metacommunicative utterance is specific in structure. Therefore a speaker alters his marking behavior when he intercalates a metacommunicative utterance. I can illustrate this idea by going back to Mrs. V.'s initial narrative in Session I.

Chapter One described how Mrs. V. intercalated a comment about Marge's behavior as she described Marge's request to be helped upstairs. Mrs. V. paused in her utterance, cocked her head slightly, lowered her eyes, and used paralanguage that indicated incredulity and disapproval. Then she said: "A young girl like her!" Then she straightened her head, looked back at Malone, and continued her narrative.

In Period 2, when Mrs. V.'s account was called in to question, she used metacommunicative points about her own behavior. These sometimes were conciliatory toward

Marge, or they offered a concession. Sometimes these point-units rationalized her own behavior.

At one point, for example, Mrs. V. said, "Well, I am, I call myself mental." (Marge had just accused her of being mentally ill.) In saying this she looked down at the floor, put her fingertips on her chest, and used an overhigh paralanguage with laughter—a configuration we interpret as embarrassment.

Many of Marge's language points were statements that commented upon what her mother said, in an insinuating or disparaging way. Marge mocked her mother's behavior in a non-vocal point. Later she whispered in a stage whisper with mocking paralanguage: "You said I ought to have good sleep and eat." Still later she said sarcastically: "Gonna go to hell." At one point she used baby talk in a mocking way. At another time she insinuated: "You know who, Mother, you know who." This statement, too, was said with a mocking smile.

Marge later performed a more spectacular form of indirect disparagement. She sat upright and said "Fongoo a la madre," making the classical obscene southern-Italian gesture of raising her right elbow with her left hand. She accompanied this point with a look of exaggerated shock, which presumably mimicked her mother's expected response.

At another time, Marge performed a point that was at least partly metacommunicative. She crossed her legs improperly and said: "Sexy, you mean, oh boy." This remark was addressed in an extrapersonal mode, over the heads of the others, to the "world at large." The referent was a remark that Whitaker had just made. At that point in the session, all the participants seemed to be making metacommunicative remarks about each other's performance: Mrs. V. said to Marge, "You're just goofy now." Whitaker said, "Sometimes I feel like an animal. Don't you feel like an animal sometimes?" Marge said, "I don't know what you're talking about." And Malone said with mock incredulity, "Really?"

Sometimes Marge would interrupt her mother's account

by saying something shocking; for example, she said, "I get sexy with myself." But she would use a shocked, outraged expression of face that I presume was a mocking imitation of her mother's past behavior. I postulate, then, that Marge's shocking behavior was a kind of dramatized commentary on behaviors that occurred in her home, and hence a behavior intermediate between direct commentary and narration.

In simple narrative and questioning, the address is direct—eye to face, or interpersonal in Birdwhistell's terms. In metacommunicative behavior, the address is directed almost anywhere else.

The address may be directed to the self. The metacommunicative speaker looks down at his own hands or body or legs. This is especially likely when he is commenting on his own behavior; we often see this arrangement in confessions of shame or guilt.

The metacommunicative address may be directed to the ceiling or to the world at large. In this case a subtle reference to someone present may be inferred and, if the shoe fits, that person can wear it. The extrapersonal address may also be aimed at a vacant chair or at a space that is not occupied. In such cases, we can often infer that some absent member is being addressed, or else some figure of the past—an "introject," in psychoanalytic terms (S. Freud, 1949; Abraham, 1949).

Marge used this form of address a great deal; I think it is quite characteristic for schizophrenic patients to do so. Such patients will often "detach" a body part, functionally speaking, and hold it out of participation. This body part will move at different rhythms from those of the rest of the body and from the movements of the other participants. It is writhed and moved or held dead, as if it lacked relation to the present. Instead, the movement seems related to some other transaction. The metacommunicative point, then, is often addressed to another behavior or to the maker of that behavior. And it is performed just after the behavior it modifies, or it is intercalated in that unit itself.

A unit of behavior is not necessarily metacommunicative or *not* metacommunicative. Any utterance, for example, occurs in a tone of voice that is metacommunicative, and each gesture and facial expression is also metacommunicative (see below). All units have metacommunicative features. When a point is obviously directed at an ongoing behavior, or is heavily loaded with metacommunicative elements, I have classed it as metacommunicative. But, more accurately, we have to generalize as follows: Any unit of behavior may contain subunits or elements that are metacommunicative to the larger unit. The metacommunicative point-unit is the subunit of some larger position in which it has a metabehavioral significance.

There are, of course, larger units that have metacommunicative relation to the stream of communicative behavior. Here, for instance, are two positions that were metacommunicative in Session I.

When Mrs. V. was narrating the family history, Marge assumed a position of huddling near her mother. In this position she carried out a lexical and kinesic commentary on what her mother said. She added statements, but tended to do so disparagingly. She muttered under-her-breath comments about what Mrs. V. said, made faces that mocked and indicated incredulity. She covertly appealed to the men for attention and created distractions by addressing the camera, sprawling on the sofa, and exhibiting her legs.

When mother and daughter turned to each other and argued, Malone would perform a brief position of intervention, which was metacommunicative in character: He would lean forward, unfold his arms, and grasp his right knee with his hands. He would then rock forward in his chair toward the women. He would speak first to Marge, commenting critically on her interruption, and then invite Mrs. V. to continue her narrative.

This position would last about ten seconds or so, just long enough for Malone to say a few sentences; then he would return to his initial baseline position of listening and questioning. This intervention is about the simplest type of position that we ordinarily observe in a conversation. It consisted only of postural shift, then a brief speech and facial expression, and then a return to the baseline posture.

The Metacommunicative Gesture

Some gestures are used with or instead of metacommunicative units of speech. Like certain words, they have a conventional reference to some lexical-cognitive context.

Although we discussed gestures in Section I as they qualified or instructed about what was then going on in the transaction, in these cases one person acted metacommunicatively toward what someone else was saying or doing.

But one can also act metacommunicatively to one's own behavior. Mrs. V., for instance, used the gesture as a metacommunicative qualifier of her own statements. When her story was challenged, she would reaffirm her veracity. She would place her right palm over her heart. This gesture is used typically in such contexts and is generally recognized, even when it occurs without comment, as an indicator of sincerity.

She also used a common gesture that I shall call nose-wiping. This gesture served as a monitor to Marge's behavior (Scheflen, 1963). The back of the index finger is brought laterally across the nostrils and upper lip. This behavior characteristically appears when a speaker lies or exaggerates or when some deviancy in non-lexical behavior occurs, such as sitting too close, exposing the legs, or being too informal.

Similarly, Marge would address the camera or one of the men and make a facial grimace. These facial configurations can also be considered gestures. They often represent the expression of ridicule, mock incredulity, anger, love, mock terror, and so forth.

Presumably the facial appearance in affective states is known in common culture and can be replicated as a deliberate commentary on what is happening. A good many of Marge's gestures were characteristically Roman Catholic. She sometimes made the sign of the cross and gesture of stabbing herself (reminiscent of contrition gestures in religious ceremonies). Once, she shook her hand from side

to side, as if shaking off a contaminant. Marge also used
the palm-on-chest gesture and two others that commonly
appear in conversation.

The participant may place his hand over his mouth. This
gesture can occur when a speaker has been told to be quiet
or when he has just uttered a prohibited or embarrassing
comment. The participant extends his lower arms and turns
his palms upward. (In eastern-European Jewish culture,
shoulder shrugging is often added.) This gesture accompanied Marge's statements of helplessness or resignation.

Mrs. V. used nose-wiping whenever Marge acted sexy
and allied with Whitaker. Whitaker would regularly light
his pipe before supporting Marge, and after a few repeti-
tions of this sequencing, Mrs. V. began to nose-wipe whenever Whitaker started to light his pipe.

After the first few minutes Malone, too, wiped his nose
when Marge acted sexy. On a half dozen occasions, Malone and Mrs. V. performed the nose-wiping point at exactly the same time.

The men used other common gestures:

1. *Eye Covering.* A hand is placed, palm inward, over
one eye. This microbehavior tends to appear in two related
contexts: (1) when a woman exhibits her legs, and (2)
when a man is trying to comprehend an elusive idea or
insight.

2. *Eye Pointing.* A participant will point to his own eye
with his index finger or place the finger on the eye. This
act often accompanies demands to pay attention or recognize an idea.

3. *Lint Picking.* The men occasionally looked down at
their bodies, then reached to their clothing and picked up
a fragment of lint with their thumb and index finger. They
then reached over and shook this off on the floor. Lint-
picking often occurs when a patient has said something that
normally would elicit censure, but the therapist, trained not
to criticize, seems to lint-pick instead.

It is ordinarily believed that the facial expression is a
genetically coded and universal human reaction. Certain
facial reactions appear early in infancy and childhood and

are probably phylogenetically old. But facial displays differ cross-culturally to some degree. They are learned (to some extent) in accordance with the traditional patterns of a cultural group. Whatever their origins, people do learn to perform facial displays *in order to* indicate their attitudes about ongoing events.

Facial displays can therefore be used as a type of commentary or metacommunicative behavior. They may accompany a metacommunicative word or point-unit. Or they may be held as a facial demeanor over longer units of communicative behavior. I will now deal with facial displays as a form of gesture.

The literature on facial communicative behavior is extensive, but consists largely of folklore. Ordinarily the facial displays of a metacommunicative type are called reactions or expressions and are named according to Western notions about the types of affect or emotion. Hence one speaks of facial expressions of terror, anxiety, hostility, rage, shame, guilt, happiness, and so on. We also speak of a class of metacommunicative facial displays that show seriousness, humor, teasing, and other qualities that indicate the credibility or literality of a statement. But the uses of the face have not yet been worked out according to the principles of structural research, so I will not comment further about them.

The Metacommunicative Use of Style and Emic Form

As I claimed earlier, the emic forms of speech and gesture and the styles of performance should identify the emic system of meaning and the institutional connotations of a speaker's meaning. But sometimes the matter is ambiguous, so a speaker emphasizes or accentuates that emic form or style which identifies his meaning; or maybe he uses a certain style or emic form for tactical reasons.

If a speaker has many institutional styles, he is likely to use a variety of styles. I believe, however, that he unwittingly stresses the styles of a particular institution when he has the meanings of that institution in mind. He may, of course, also do this on purpose.

Sometimes a participant will exaggerate or put on a certain institutional style to show his identification with a certain institutional group. He may do this, for example, to increase his rapport with them or to curry their political favor. By the same token, certain acculturated foreigners again use the language forms of their native country when they go home for a visit. Emic forms are also used to increase understanding and rapport or show cultural preferences. Obviously, a participant of multicultural and multi-institutional experience can also use form and style in a metacommunicative way in order to conceal his origins and his meanings or to mislead other people about them.

The References of Metacommunicative Behavior

In summary, a participant can qualify his own communicative behavior by altering his marking behavior, adding statements or gestures, and/or by changing his paracommunicative style or form. There is nothing characteristic about the morphology of metacommunicative behaviors. Though there are special markers of their occurrence, they are classed as metacommunicative because they have reference to the ongoing systems of communicative behavior, and in one way or another qualify, modify, or specify these. So I am not postulating a morphological class of metacommunicative behavior, although I will do so in Chapter Ten, when metacommunicative acts not related to language are described. Instead, we are dealing with a particular logical type of behavioral relations—a relation in which one unit of behavior refers to another as a kind of commentary.

The unit of behavior that is used metacommunicatively refers to an immediately ongoing stream of activity as well as to some concept or idea. The remote referent of a metacommunicative act is some rule of procedure or conduct or some value or judgmental standard. The metacommunicative act comments upon and makes at least an implied judgment about the veracity or literalness or correctness or allowability of the behaviors of the immediate present. Thus the referential system of metacommunicative behavior is some institutionally held and culturally transmitted infrasystem of standards and values.

In any event, a participant in communication can enact the customary behaviors of speech in order to depict an idea and can comment or make facial and hand displays about these values of this behavior, as I have described here.

In fact, a participant has a variety of options, at least in theory. He can: (1) act or think metacommunicatively about his own performance as he acts communicatively, or (2) think or act metacommunicatively instead of speaking in narration or explanation, or (3) act metacommunicatively toward someone else's performance and thereby change, interdict, correct, or qualify it.

Metacommunicative behavior, then, can be used to change, conceal, rationalize, or otherwise manage human behavior. In any of these events, the performance of any metacommunicative act adds information about the communicative processes in progress. The metacommunicative supplement may thereby specify contexts and clarify a performance—or it may further increase ambiguities and diminish the ability to arrive at meaning.

Chapter Nine

The Bowl

Some metacommunicational behaviors or signals play a role in the progression of complex programs such as the psychotherapy sessions. One of these previously mentioned is a gesture I will call the "bowl." The bowl gesture was of significance in all the Whitaker-Malone sessions. This gesture proved to be a metacommunicative act that at one and the same time was (1) an icon to illustrate a lexical unit, (2) a metacommunicative gesture signaling the non-literality of a meaning, and (3) a signal to alter the relationships of the transaction.

The Bowl Gesture and Its Immediate Contexts

During a session of the Whitaker-Malone series with Marge, Malone moved forward in his chair toward Marge, made a bowl-shaped gesture with his hands, and addressed her as follows:

> I had the first mind-picture (daydream) I had with you. Right then. It was a beautiful gold tray, like the kind they make in India with the little pretty designs in it . . . that are carved in it. A beautiful tray about this big around (a foot in diameter, as judged by his gesture). It had a whole lot of fruit . . . it was so pretty; but when I went over to it . . . it was artificial . . . but it was still pretty . . . and I picked up the apple that was on top . . . and I . . . right under the apple was a pile of shit. And then the thought occurred to me was that. . . . Oh, I went to hell with you when

I saw that picture. . . . I don't know what way. . . .
Just telling you what my thoughts are.

FIGURE 9-1.   Malone performing the bowl gesture

If we are to study a communicative behavior, we must
have a number of instances of it to compare in order to
see if we are dealing with a customary, traditional act.
Then we must know if this act occurs each time in similar
contexts and therefore has a customary, established meaning. I searched all of the psychotherapy films we had, to
see if I could find other occurrences of this bowl gesture.

I found that there were other bowl gestures in other sessions of the therapy with Marge. There was also one in
a session with a schizophrenic man Whitaker and Malone
treated at Temple. In 1964 we had gone to Atlanta and
filmed Whitaker, Malone, and two of their associates. Each
of these other men also made the bowl gesture; in fact,
two of the patients also made the gesture.

Since I found this gesture occurring again and again in
sessions conducted by Whitaker and his associates and I
had not seen it elsewhere, I first jumped to the mistaken
conclusion that the gesture was peculiar to the method that
these psychotherapists had developed.

But, since the time of this study, I have noticed a variety
of other people using the "bowl" in the same context. An

interesting experience in studying non-lexical behavior is
that once you have studied one particular movement,
though you never noticed it before, you then see it everywhere. It appears that we are not conscious of the most
ordinary kinesic activities until special experience changes
our awareness. My guess is that the bowl gesture is very
common in American body language in the special circumstances I will describe.

I noticed that the bowls occurred at nineteen minutes
after the start of each session and at no other time or place.
This patterning seemed to suggest that they were recurrences of a single unit. But then I also noted differences
in each occurrence. Malone performed two of them and
Whitaker one. In addition, in one of the recurrences it was
the girl who talked, rather than the performer of the bowl.
The bowl actions in Sessions I and III were briefer in duration that those in Session IX.

The difference brought up a crucial question in research
methodology: *Are these variations merely style differences
in the performance of one standard unit? Or are they in
fact just many kinds of behaviors, some of which happen
to look alike?*

I did not attempt to find the answer by speculation. Here
is the principle: If two actions have the same function each
time—that is, if they appear in the same contexts over and
over—they are allomorphs, or emes (Pike, 1954), or substitutable variants—not different units. Said otherwise, a
standard unit is defined as one that has the same morphology and the same function or situations of occurrence.
So unless I move on to examining the contexts of the bowl
gestures, I cannot know any more about their significance.

Behaviors That Occurred with the Bowl Gesture
With each bowl gesture, there occurred a characteristic
configuration of other behaviors:

1 *Attention and Orientation Actions by Others.*
During Malone's bowl action in Session IX, Whitaker
and the girl signaled attentiveness by the usual devices, e.g.,

head cocking, remaining silent, looking at the speaker, slightly widening the eyelid aperture, and so on.

Communicative units are rarely performed by only one person when others are also present who know the routine. At the very least, the others will indicate attentiveness/inattentiveness, comprehension/incomprehension, and so forth, thereby influencing the pacing, detail, and continuance of a performance. But usually they participate in a unit even more actively. Two or more will perform conjointly the basic component behaviors of the unit, often in complementarity (Bateson, 1958; Haley, 1963), as when one speaker starts a sentence and another finishes it. In fact, when in a pattern a given behavior is called for at a certain point, it may not matter who performs it. If it is performed, the sequence continues; if it is not, the pattern repeats, halts, or takes another direction.

When you are familiar with pattern, you learn that some variations make no difference. You might have guessed that the minor variations in the bowl performances in the three sessions were not significant. This proved to be the case. At one level, it did not matter whether it was Whitaker or Malone who made the bowl or who spoke during its performance.[1]

As we will see in the next chapter, this did not happen with the bowl gesture in Session IX, and considerable deviation was associated with its non-occurrence. There was a characteristic orientating behavior on the girl's part when one of the men made the bowl gesture. She smiled at him, uncrossed her legs, and turned her body to him.

2 Seductive-type Behaviors by Marge

Bowl behavior in every case was preceded by a characteristic action on the girl's part. Kinesically, she behaved

---

[1] It may make a difference who performs a given unit when that person has a special status. For instance, a monitor may not correct a deviancy unless it is performed by a high-status figure. But even though the identity of the performer makes no difference at some level—that is, the pattern continues unchanged—the difference may appear at some much higher level. For example, the group members may continue the meeting but later express dissatisfaction at who performed what and perhaps not attend further meetings.

in a somewhat seductive or flirtatious way. But due to the addition of certain other kinesics, these actions appeared as a parody of seductiveness. In each case, she was talking about sex in a more or less tasteless way. The total configuration was a kind of gross parody of seductiveness. An example is shown in Figure 9-2.

FIGURE 9-2.   Marge in seductive-type behavior

This behavior, occurring immediately before the bowl gesture, would be thought of as a cue in an interactional view. Her action during the bowl—she sat motionless, deadpan—might be considered a response. We might conjecture that the pseudoseductive cue *caused* the bowl, which in turn *caused* the deadpan, and so on. This model, in which one person's response is the stimulus to another's behavior, is very popular these days. In disagreement with this model, I would suggest that such interactional sequences trigger and regulate the steps in a communicational program; they do not cause them. Here I will look at such accompanying behavior as part of the context of the bowl behavior.

3 *A Characteristic Lexical Content: Relating a Fantasy*
At each bowl, the speaker was relating a fantasy, or daydream. I checked this out for the other five bowls that I found in the films of Whitaker, Malone, and their Atlanta associates. On every occasion, the speaker was telling a

daydream, or fantasy, he had had about one of the other people present. If the speaker does not make the bowl gesture, someone else present does so. It is a purposive tactic in the Whitaker school to tell the patient a fantasy the therapist had about him.[2] By psychodynamic inference, we could speculate that in each case the fantasy concerned forbidden sexuality. In Session I, when Malone made the bowl, the girl was talking about daydreaming that her parents were struggling in bed. In Session III, Whitaker said he had hoped Marge could be a little girl, since she was unable to be a woman. Then he added that he imagined her as a rag doll left out in the rain that needed to be washed. Malone added that she smelled and was dirty.

4 Pipe Lighting

Just before, during, or after the bowl action, one or both therapists lit their pipes.

5 A Characteristic Pattern of Postural Shifts

Every bowl action was initiated and terminated with exactly the same shifts in bodily posture (with one interesting and revealing exception in Session IX, which will be described below). These postural shifts consisted of the following actions: a At the beginning of each bowl, the performer tilted his head slightly to the right, looked at the girl, shifted his pipe to the left side of his mouth, and brought his arms to his lap. b For the duration of the bowl action, he kept the backs of his hands resting in his lap. c At the end of the bowl sequence and fantasy, he moved toward the patient, brought his head back to the erect position, uncrossed his legs, and took his pipe in his left hand.

There was a special feature of the postural configuration of the bowl unit that appeared nowhere else in any session: From the beginning of each session until the nineteenth minute, when the bowl gesture was made, the performer

---

[2] In the volume *Strategy and Structure in Psychotherapy*, a psychoanalytic analysis of this behavior is also published. There is also a context analysis of the lexical behavior of all of the sessions. Thus in taking this portion of the book for republication, I have taken the analysis of the bowl gesture out of its clinical contexts.

of the bowl held his pipe in his *right* hand. When he formed the bowl, he had to let go of his pipe. During the gesture, he held it in his mouth. At the end of the bowl performance, he took hold of his pipe with his *left* hand and continued to hold it in his left hand until six minutes later, when he made physical contact with the patient.

In other words, a postural shift occurred with the bowl unit that proved to be a marker for a still larger unit. In one postural shift, then, we see the initiation of a unit and of a larger unit, comparable to the way a starting gun might signal the beginning of a lap, a race, or a racing season. So extensive a shift marker tips us off that some important point of reorientation is occurring in the interaction.

Thus a postural marker also can instruct participants what to do and when to do it. It can have yet another function; it can indicate how a given action is to be regarded—whether, for instance, a statement is to be taken literally or figuratively. Any action when seen as an indicator of this type can be called a *metasignal* (Bateson, 1955). As we will see, the bowl gesture functioned in the larger bowl unit as a signal that what was being said was to be taken as a fantasy, or daydream. Analogously, the posture "left-hand-on-pipe" will tell us how certain courting-like behaviors that occurred only during this posture are to be taken. Thus in at least these two ways— whether we see them as markers or as metasignals—postural activities serve to orient participants in an interaction.

But let us get back to the task of building our hierarchy. The bowl gesture occurred each time in the same configuration: Marge's seductive-type behavior, relating a daydream, postural shifting, and so on. This is how patterned human behavior is. These configurations are no more stereotyped than other interactions we have studied. The question now becomes: Which of these behaviors are units at the same level and constitute the components of the next larger unit? To know this, we must know more about their relations to each other. It is not enough to know merely that they co-occurred, or were simultaneous in time.

A shift in the posture of Malone's entire body was involved in making the bowl unit. He moved forward toward Marge as he started this unit of action, and he moved back away from her and crossed his legs after he had completed it.

Suppose we pay special attention to this marking behavior (I will come back to the other contextual features of the unit later). You will note that pipe lighting and the attention-orientation behaviors that co-occurred, or correlated in time, with the bowl gesture did not prove to be interdependent; i.e., they did not *have* to occur. This unit, which I will call the bowl unit, could be diagramed as follows:

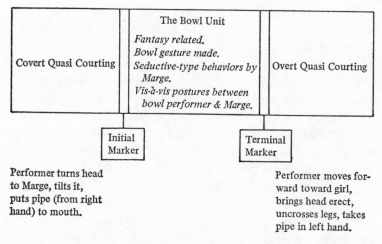

FIGURE 9-3.   The bowl unit

Larger Units to Which the Bowl Unit Belonged

As noted in previous chapters, quasi-courting interactions superficially resemble courtship in that they contain elements such as flirtatious and appealing gestures, vis-à-vis postures, and brief tactile contacts that ordinarily appear in courtship. But such sequences are differentiated by "qualifying" behaviors that show actual courtship is not in progress. Quasi courting is generally postural, kinesic, and tactile, and generally is performed unawares by the participants. It functions in interactions not to set up seduction but, rather, to define gender, to increase the attentiveness of participants, and in general to establish and maintain relatedness and rapport.

Covert quasi-courting behavior is regular in psychotherapy and can be thought of as in the service of establishing rapport. In the Whitaker-Malone sessions, it consisted of tête-à-tête positioning, handkerchief waving, preening, exchanging glances, and so on. It took this covert form until the nineteenth minute of each session—when the bowl unit occurred—and returned to this form in the terminal minute of each session. However, after the bowl unit, the quasi courting became *overt*. The flirtatious behavior became obvious, the tête-à-tête positioning was clear and uncluttered, and sexuality was discussed openly. This overt quasi courting seemed to be used consciously and purposely by these therapists as a technique to deal with certain of the girl's problems about sexuality and relationship. The overt form of quasi courting began with the bowl unit in each session and ended with an actual exchange of tactile behaviors between the quasi-courting therapist and the girl. Dr. English describes in his chapter one of these occasions of contacting, when the girl was asked to rub Malone's foot as he had rubbed hers.

There was a sequence in time, then, of the units covert quasi courting: overt quasi courting. *The bowl unit marked the transition from the covert to the overt form.* Overt quasi courting invariably led to contacting. This sequence is shown in Figure 9-4.

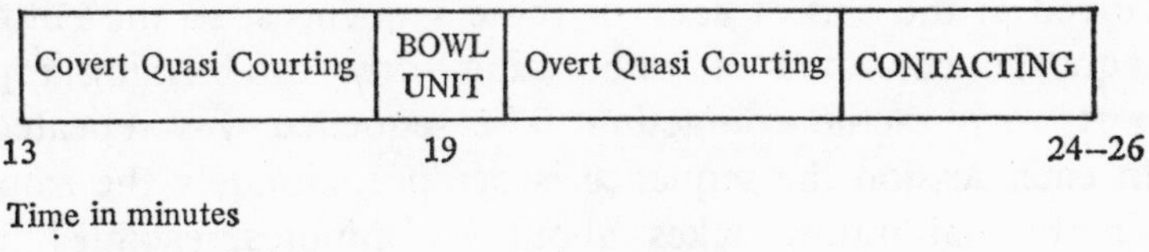

Covert Quasi Courting	BOWL UNIT	Overt Quasi Courting	CONTACTING
13	19		24–26

Time in minutes

FIGURE 9-4. Total quasi-courting unit

Structurally, the bowl unit belonged to the larger unit, covert quasi courting, which, together with overt quasi courting (and contacting), made up the still larger quasi-courting unit.

The bowl gesture occurred with the recounting of a day-dream, or fantasy. This combination—the bowl gesture and a fantasy—occurred at a time when the patient shifted from a pattern of covert quasi courting to an overt quasi courting. But this shift was not an activity that Marge alone was engaged in. Both men were involved; they shifted their tactics at this point. Thus the bowl unit occurred at the beginning of a phase in the session—a phase when all three of the participants initiated a different structure of relationships. I assume that this is why any one of them could perform the bowl gesture. If a given signal is necessary to mark a shift in relationships or activities, it may not matter *who* performs it.

In the format of the psychotherapy session, there is a characteristic shift in the therapist's orientation and relationship to the patient. He begins a session in a position of relative non-involvement and constraint—sitting back, listening, and encouraging the patient to speak about his problems. Then, at some point he will move forward toward the patient, increase his involvement, and attempt to establish rapport. Elsewhere I have called these units of tactical behavior "elaborating" and "establishing rapport," respectively (Scheflen, 1973).

Like many other psychotherapists, Whitaker and Malone carry out this sequence of shifting from elaborating to establishing rapport twice in each session. The second of these shifts is the more intensive and well developed. In the Whitaker-Malone approach, a brief tactile contact occurred at the end of each of these sequences, so the entire sequence consisted of elaborating, *then* establishing rapport, *then* tactile contacting. The sequence was repeated. In each session the sequence is of approximately the same length; elaborating takes about six minutes, establishing rapport another six or so. Contacting lasted about a minute or two. The entire sequence required about twelve to thirteen minutes for each repetition.

These sequences of unit performance are diagramed in

Figure 9-5. The reader can see that the bowl unit occurred each time in the second repetition, when the therapist made his second shift from elaborating to establishing rapport.

First Occurrence   Second Occurrence

			BOWL	
		CONTACT	UNIT	CONTACT
LARGELY KINESIC UNITS	Covert Quasi Courting	Covert Quasi Courting	Covert Quasi Courting	Overt Quasi Courting	
LARGELY LEXICAL UNITS	Elaborating	Establishing Rapport	Elaborating	Establishing Rapport	

PERIOD OF INTRODUCTION

PERIOD OF TERMINATION

O Pipe lighting

6   12–13   19   25–÷

Time in minutes

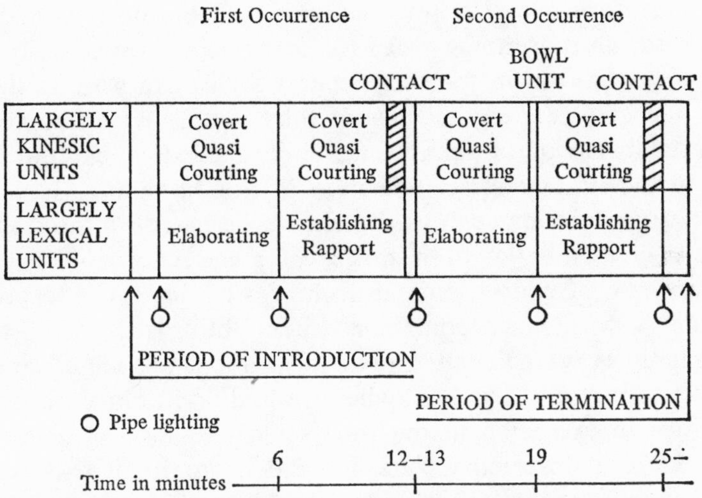

FIGURE 9-5.   Program of Whitaker-Malone-Marge session

Thus, the occurrence of the bowl unit marked a simultaneous shift in two kinds of communicational activity: from covert to overt quasi-courting behavior and from elaborating to establishing rapport.

Technically speaking, these two patterns of behavior constitute separate units of behavior (Scheflen, 1973), but they are coterminous and interdependent. I think that quasi-courting behavior is part of the behavioral relatedness in established rapport.

We can make a preliminary formulation about the communicational function of the bowl unit. It occurs at the transition between listening to the patient's narrative and the unit of establishing rapport. It seems to signal that the daydream and the shift into courtship-like behavior are to be taken as metaphorical rather than literal actions. Thus as the lexical statement is metasignaled as a fantasy, the courtship-like activities are metasignaled as some form of play, practice, or exploration. We could assume that placing such a metaphorical value upon the activities allows them to happen.

A Variation in the Bowl Unit

On every occasion but one, at which the bowl unit occurred, its morphology was the same as I have described, and it occurred in the same contexts. We can assume that it had a regular significance in this system of communicational behavior, a significance I have tried to capture as a metacommunicative indication of non-literality.

An abstraction such as this should be based on the study of a great number of instances of great regularity. There were not, of course, enough instances of this event to provide us with much confidence about the formulation. But sometimes we can tell a great deal about the significance of a communicational act when we find an instance of variation—an exception to the rule, so to speak.

Such an instructive variation did occur in one session. Malone introduced deviation into his performance of the unit. He lit his pipe, uncrossed his arms and legs, made the bowl gesture, and verbalized the fantasy of the fruit and bowl, but when he had finished, he recrossed his arms and legs and moved back in his chair *instead of moving in* toward Marge and carrying on the overt quasi courting. His tone of voice was particularly icy, and he also began the unit with an unusual kinesic action: he turned his head abruptly away from the girl as he began to address her. This is an action that breaks contact in a conversation, and it is of some consequence that Malone does this at the moment he is presumably trying to *initiate* conversation.

Whitaker did not play his expected part in the bowl unit. He did not answer Malone's pipe-lighting signal, and he did not move in the rapport position, as was expected at this point. Rather, he turned away from Marge, toward the research observers, put his feet up on the coffee table, and fell into a motionless and expressionless attitude.

Marge also failed to play her part. She withheld the seductive behavior that signaled her readiness to move into overt quasi courting. She had to be prompted to do so.

When Malone addressed her, she did not move or show expression. She started to turn to him, and she did uncross her legs as usual, but she immediately recrossed them. She appeared pained and depressed, instead of smiling as she usually did.

In short, the bowl unit did not come off and advance the program into rapport and overt quasi courting. From a cultural viewpoint, the progression was held up for four minutes. From a social standpoint, the interrelations of the group appeared to have broken down—the members appeared detached, dislocated, and disinterested, and they withheld their usual responses to each other.

The quasi-courting cue before the bowl and the relationships during its performance had a perfunctory and detached quality. In fact, it was like this throughout the ninth session. For example: At the contacting step at twelve minutes, the men had to urge Marge to participate, just as they had to prompt her to cue the bowl unit. She responded with much resisting and complaining. The girl was remote and flippant throughout the session. She talked a good deal more than usual, but in an offhand, distant way. She seemed to be in better contact in this session than in previous sessions. She seemed less psychotic, and her readiness for quasi courting seemed markedly reduced. In other sessions, the men often had to stop her seductive activities.

The men, too, held back. Malone used the head-turning avoidance. He sometimes turned away when she looked at him. Whitaker was more detached and remote than in other sessions. This mutual detachment was verbalized. The men criticized Marge for her detachment and indifference and for the unattractive quality of some of her quasi courting. It seems to me that such criticism was the gist of Malone's fantasy.

In any program, the manner, the tone and quality with which the steps are carried out, is obviously important. Such qualities are what people are trying to identify when they say that a partner is not "giving." They are complaining that he will not perform the expected steps or that he performs them without affect or enthusiasm. Such lack of affect or hostility can lead to the breakdown of a program, or at least to delays in its progress. This is an example of how a cultural and a psychological view supplement each other.

The quality of the quasi courting was set up or signaled in the earliest interchanges of the session. This is a reliable finding in any interaction: the first minute gives indication of what is to come. The initial alignments are usually stable and the early behaviors rehearse and signal the interaction. In Session IX the initial quasi courting showed a drastic deviation from the other sessions.

In the beginning of every session, there was a preening routine between Marge and the quasi-courting therapist. In Session IX there was an unexpected twist. Malone straightened his tie and pulled up his socks; Marge adjusted her sweater, opened it to expose her protruded chest, set her leg posture for best exhibition, and so on. *But Malone was watching an attractive secretary walk across the room* (in violation, of course, of all the plans for filming). He was not looking at Marge at all. When he turned to her and saw her watching him and preening for him, he abruptly turned his head away from her, as he did just before the bowl point at nineteen minutes, and *yawned very ostentatiously.*

This action served as a clear qualifying signal about his relationship to Marge. It was not to be an attentive or excluding one-to-one or quasi courtship. And Marge responded in kind: She immediately dissociated herself, also looking away, and told Malone that she had a case on a male assistant.

Variations in the Rapport Unit

If you will recall, the bowl unit and the shift into overt quasi courting (the kinesic units) originally occurred at the time the lexically active therapists moved into the rapport unit with the patient. Whitaker, the lexically active therapist in this session, should have answered Malone's pipe-lighting signal and moved into rapport with, and support of, Marge. Instead, Whitaker turned from the girl, placed his feet up on the coffee table, and became motionless and expressionless.

The pipe-lighting interchange that should have initiated the rapport also failed to come off. First of all, Whitaker did not "answer" Malone's nineteenth-minute pipe lighting (immediately before the bowl unit began) until four minutes later. He took out, filled, and tamped his pipe, but did not light it.

Second, both men accompanied their pipe behavior with a strange activity. When Malone finished lighting his pipe, he shook his hand violently as if to shake loose a clinging bit of tobacco. Whitaker looked away from Malone, tamped his pipe, and then, holding his hand high in the air, also shook it and flicked his fingers violently and repeatedly, also as if to remove an adhering foreign object. So exhibitionistically was this done that it struck me as some kind of a signal. It was then that Whitaker moved to face away from the girl and put his feet up on the coffee table.

This flicking and waving behavior occurred on two other occasions when Whitaker delayed his move-in. This action and his turning away from the girl seemed to be a signal that he was not prepared to light his pipe and move in.

Malone's hand waving looked like a signal of nullification, as if he no sooner started the bowl when he thought better of it. If this was the case, the incident fitted in with a phenomenon that is common in carrying out a program. An interactant may start to carry out a step even though he consciously decides not to or says he will not do so. We all have had this experience. Remember how in a long-standing relationship certain unfavorable sequences sometimes get going and lead to trouble. You may anticipate your own unfavorable contribution and determine to behave differently, only to catch yourself going ahead and playing your familiar part.

Psychologically speaking, much of the behavior in a program is unconscious. This is advantageous in allowing many behaviors to be carried out efficiently and automatically, but it has the disadvantage of leaving some actions outside conscious control. Often, then, a participant goes ahead with the kinesic and postural activities of the program even though he withholds the conscious linguistic parts or modifies them in accordance with a contingency that has demanded a modification. This is my guess about what Malone did. He had automatically begun the bowl unit and then felt he should not go ahead under the circumstances. So he did not move in.

Variations in the Total Program

The variation in performance of the bowl in Session IX was reflected in variations in many aspects of the program: the introductory qualifying signal about the quasi courting and the subsequent quality of the quasi courting, the failure of the rapport relationship to be developed, and the general signals of nullification and hesitancy. In addition, the men seemed to be out of phase throughout the session. At twelve minutes, for example, Malone moved into contact with the girl, when the previous signals indicated that Whitaker would do so. In general, the men interrupted each other's relationship with Marge and often had to look toward each other, presumably for cues—an inco-ordination that I did not see in any other session they conducted. Clearly, some problem was evident in the performance of the entire program in Session IX.

This became very clear in the four minutes after the bowl unit failed of completion, that is, in the four minutes that Whitaker withheld his pipe lighting. A startling thing happened. *One of the observers* moved into the picture and performed a modified bowl unit. Then Whitaker took over and told the girl a fantasy. It was as though, since Malone, with his bowl gesture and accompanying fantasy, failed to advance the program, two other men tried their hand. Here, in some detail, is what happened:

At exactly the moment Malone moved out instead of in, a research observer moved forward directly into the center of the camera's field and occupied the center of the film for two minutes. Whitaker, Malone, and the girl watched him—motionless. The girl grinned. The observer held up a notebook on which he had been writing. Clearly recorded by the camera were the words "Fruit of the Womb." Then he folded the notebook, moved back, and crossed his arms and legs, just as Malone had done.

This observer did not realize he was on camera, nor did he think of himself as performing in the Whitaker-Malone sessions. Consciously he thought he wanted to convey his fantasy about the therapy to the woman observer sitting behind him. (Malone had done something like this with the male schizophrenic patient they had also been seeing. He allowed him to leave, then turned to an observer and, with accompanying bowl gesture, told a fantasy he had had about the patient.)

The observer's bowl unit was not directed to Marge, and the observer did not move in on her. But, otherwise, the performance was structurally like a bowl unit. It had the usual markers and occurred in the correct context. Although written content was substituted, the way the notebook was held in the air duplicated remarkably the hand position in the bowl unit. It will not escape you that the words "Fruit of the Womb" resemble the tray of fruit Malone alluded to in his bowl unit.

I do not want to give the impression that the observer forced himself unannounced or uninvited into the picture; this is not at all the case. Whether they realized it or not, it seemed that all the participants—even the cameraman— were party to this observer's participation.

Whitaker had positioned himself, just before Malone's bowl unit, in such a manner as to include the observer in the threesome. And the cameraman unwittingly shifted the camera just a bit, to center him on the film. When the observer moved in, Whitaker, Malone, and the girl turned and watched him.

The point is that when a step is called for in a program, if one person fails to perform it another person will, and if one's performance does not come off, someone else may repeat it so that the step will be completed and the group can go on in its task.

Whitaker in fact intervened at the end of the observer's

action and brought the session to an end. I have elsewhere described a complex set of contextual circumstances that obtained in this ninth session—circumstances that seemed to explain why Whitaker and the girl did not participate in the behaviors that usually surrounded the bowl unit. In brief, Whitaker and the girl were operating in a definition of the situation that precluded the occurrence of quasi courting and rapport in that session. Thus we could generalize that a customary metasignal will not have its customary significance and effect if it occurs in some other, unexpected context.

Chapter Ten

Signals and Commands

A gesture or stylistic exaggeration or comment can be addressed to someone in a particular manner and thus serve as an instruction or order. Most such metacommunicative acts are directed at the performances and relationships of group members; they do not, therefore, qualify language behavior directly. But they may alter the transactional context of a meaning and thus qualify it indirectly.

Signals

Often a participant makes a face or gesticulates a response that he does not address to anyone in particular or exhibit to the others. He may, in fact, conceal this metacommunicative reaction by turning his face away from the others or by covering his face with his hands.

But, on other occasions, a participant displays his metacommunicative gesture. He seems to be deliberately showing others how he feels about their actions or speech. To do this, he may jut his face or jaw toward them or make a sound that attracts their attention. Or he may place his finger or hand on someone until he pays attention to him, and then make a metacommunicative gesture or facial display. In cases like these, where a gesture is displayed, the performer will often address his reaction explicitly. He looks at the object of his kinesic comment in a direct, eye-to-eye confrontation, gains the attention of the listener, and then makes the facial gesture; or he turns to the object, brings his hands out in front of him, points them, and then makes a hand gesture.

When gestures are directly oriented and addressed in this manner, I will speak of them as signals. In the technical language of Section I, a participant assembles the address of a point or a position and then enacts a gesture. He can do this in any degree of directness from covert to exhibitionistic and any degree of aggressiveness from embarrassed submissiveness to a full dominance display. Since a gesture can be performed in ascending degrees of directness, I will not try to establish a cutoff point at which a gesture becomes a signal. I must leave the matter relative until we have more data.

Almost any of the common gestures are sometimes actively addressed. Here are a few examples: A person may address someone and show any of a variety of common facial displays. He may also shrug his shoulders and raise his palms, hide his eyes with his hands, slap his forehead with a palm, or otherwise comment kinesically. He thus indicates an attitude rather directly.

Other addressed kinesic acts seem intended to warn a fellow participant and ward off his expected behavior. The high sign is an example. Another form of such behavior directs the attention of a speaker to some person he has presumably forgotten. This person's inattentiveness or anger may be increasing without the speaker's being aware. Or the object of a signaled reference may be a symbolic item of décor or a symbolic portrait that represents rules or principles the speaker is overlooking.

If a participant deviates from a cultural norm in the performance of his part, some other participant may make a metacommunicative remark. But there are several kinesic signals that seem to have the same monitoring significance. They appear at a time of lying, exaggeration, or other deviation in behavior, and their appearance often results in an immediate rectification of the deviance. The frown and the wiping of the index finger under the nostril are two common monitors of this type. I have described these behaviors in context elsewhere (Scheflen, 1963).

To indicate a wish to speak, participants often sit forward and erect in their chairs, address the intended auditors, place a hand or prop in the space in front of them, and make a sound. They may clear their throats, cough, or utter paralinguistic sounds or beginning sentences.

To elicit an address, participants may also sit forward and more erect, turn their heads slightly, and look at the others from the "corners" of their eyes. Women may present the palm or escalate the entire quasi-courting or courtship display. Men may use dominance behavior. Members of both sexes may fidget or move a hand or foot rapidly. And people may also move into congruent postures and synchronous movements with a speaker and thus solicit an address (Kendon, 1968).

An address is often elicited by indicating dissociation from an existing partner. To do this, one backs away, turns out of the vis-á-vis orientation, folds his arms and/or crosses his legs, looks down, falls into deadpan expression, and casts short, searching glances to a prospect who might intervene. This posture we have often called "closed." It is also used by strangers or others who are not ready for engagement or involvement (Scheflen, 1966B). A closed posture is characterized by crossed extremities, a maximum interpersonal distance, and an averting of the body from the vis-à-vis relation.

From such a closed position, a participant indicates his readiness for involvement by uncrossing his extremities, moving forward toward his vis-à-vis, and turning more fully into the direct torso-and-face orientation. These two positions on the spectrum of readiness for involvement are contrasted in Figure 10-1.

A readiness for alliance can also be signaled. Moving into a side-by-side relation or into postural congruence is a common way. Marge did this very dramatically in Session I. She stood up and sat down again nearer to Whitaker and in the posture Whitaker was using. This dramatic shift is shown in Figure 10-2.

In Chapter One I described some actonic activities that were used as signals. I said, for instance, that Marge stroked her legs sensuously while she looked alternately at

Whitaker open

Whitaker closed

FIGURE 10-1.   Whitaker in "open" and in "closed" postures toward Marge.[1]

one of the men and at her legs. The men also used pipe lighting as a co-ordinating signal.

Whitaker and Malone moved toward greater involvement with Marge every six minutes in all the psychother-

[1] This plate is reprinted from *Stream and Structure of Communicational Behavior, supra.*

FIGURE 10-2.   Marge's positional juncture[2]

apy sessions they conducted with her. Just before each move of this kind, the therapist who would make it would light his pipe. Then the other therapist would also light his pipe or puff on it ostentatiously if it was already lighted. When both pipes had been lighted, and only then, the therapist moved forward toward greater involvement and rapport. It was as though the moving-in tactic was cleared by one partner with the other.

Neither of the men was aware of this use of pipe lighting. But neither man made this move until the other had lighted up or puffed smoke. And the men did not light their pipes at times other than when they were shifting position,

[2] This plate reprinted from *The Communicational Analysis of a Transaction, supra.*

so the signal preceded each step of their strategic program (Scheflen, 1973). I would not claim, however, that they lighted their pipes in order to form a signal. It seems, rather, that a regular and predictable behavior comes to serve as an indicator or signal. By the same token, its non-occurrence may come to indicate that something is wrong or lacking and thereby serve to forestall an expected activity.

In established relationships, where the same programs of behavior are often repeated, complex units of behavior may come to be successively abbreviated. In time, then, a simple utterance or kinesic act may come to represent an entire communicative or metacommunicative unit.

Here is an example, from a psychotherapy session, that could be observed in its developmental phases: In the early sessions, the psychotherapist often commented to the patient to remind him that he was supposed to say anything that came into his mind. Whenever the therapist verbalized this admonition, he cleared his throat.

After a few sessions, the therapist simply cleared his throat without verbalizing the instruction. This representative act seemed quite sufficient, for the patient would stop talking about incidental matters and get down to reminiscing about his childhood whenever the throat clearing occurred. At a later session when the patient was small-talking, he cleared his own throat, immediately broke off this topic, and began to talk about his childhood.

Here is another example, which I observed in some films loaned to me by Dr. Margaret Bullowa of the Massachusetts Institute of Technology. Dr. Bullowa had taken films of the washing of babies at various stages in their development (Bullowa, Jones, and Duckert, 1964).

One sequence showed a little girl being bathed by her mother at three-month intervals, into her third year of life. In the early films the mother had engaged each time in a very unpleasant ritual. After she dried the baby, she insisted on inserting a Q-tips applicator into each of the baby's ears, though the child screamed and resisted the procedure violently.

By the second year, the baby had learned to wash her-self under the mother's close supervision. And fortunately the Q-Tips event had been omitted from the ceremony. But each time, when the drying was finished, the baby put her index finger into one, then the other, of her ears.

Commands and Confrontations

In most commands, the speaker turns his body fully to-ward the addressee and looks at his face in an eye-to-eye confrontation. Then he utters an imperative or a rhetorical question. Sometimes he also makes a gesture. Thus the en-tire body is likely to be involved and oriented into a full vis-à-vis with the addressee. A full shift in position is often employed for a command.

A number of primary stresses may be added to the im-perative. In addition, the head may be nodded toward the addressee, and a finger or sometimes a foot may be pointed to him. Sometimes the jaw is jutted toward the addressee at the terminal juncture, or the terminal may be stressed by an emphatic lowering of the head, hand, or fist. Some-times the command is completed by the entire presentation. Whitaker is shown exaggerating the point markers of a question in Figure 10-3.

The addressee of a command may be touched in a par-ticular way. In fact, a tactile behavior may replace the ut-

FIGURE 10-3.   Head protrusion by Whitaker on asking a ques-tion

tered command. Here is a common usage: When someone is seeking to gain the floor in a conversation, he may be touched as an instruction to remain silent. This touch is usually carried out by placing a palm on his shoulder, hand, forearm, or occasionally his knee, and pressing down slightly. A patting movement may be added, especially if the would-be speaker has already been insulted or slighted in an obvious way.

The index finger may also be used as a silencing instruction. It is pressed into the shoulder or the fossa of the elbow. Here is an example from a psychotherapy session (Scheflen, 1960), which also shows a tactile signal that seemed to initiate speech:

The patient was a young schizophrenic woman who was just beginning to recover from a very disturbed state. Her psychotherapist was showing a group of visitors that she had improved. He was seated next to his patient on a sofa. He had his right arm around her shoulder, and his left hand held her left wrist. This position gave the therapist two points of tactile contact with the patient, which he used repeatedly. When she fell silent, he gently stroked her left wrist with his left hand. Each time he did this, she began to talk. As she began to talk, she would speak more and more rapidly and excitedly. Then the therapist would press his right index finger into her right shoulder and she would fall silent.

In psychotherapy, confrontations are made in this form. The therapist assembles this form of address and makes a metacommunicative comment about the patient's behavior or personality patterns. He may or may not add a command or instruction to change.

In fact, the postural arrangements in which the bowl unit occurred were quite the same as those Malone had used in Session I when he intervened to silence Marge.

On ten occasions in Session I when Marge had interrupted her mother, Malone rocked forward from his position of listening, to confront Marge. He would gently scold her or criticize what she had said, then glance to Mrs. V.

and invite the mother to continue her narrative. This behavior is depicted in Figure 10-4.

FIGURE 10-4.   Malone's confrontation.[3]

I think this form of positional unit is used in confrontations and forceful instructions in all kinds of situations. In fact, the only unique feature of the confrontation in psychotherapy seems to be the kind of commentary that is made.

Malone's interventions usually followed and were occasioned by Marge's interruptions of her mother. In these interruptions Marge used a kind of indirect metacommunicative confrontation. She addressed this interruptive behavior to the camera or to Whitaker, but in context her utterance had an obvious though indirect reference to what her mother had just said.

Some of Marge's interruptions, as we have seen, consisted of statements that were very provocative. On such occasions Marge would perform a rather spectacular and exaggerated marking behavior. She would stand up, make her comment, then sit down. Thus she made point types of utterance in the exaggerated marking system of the position. An example of Marge's "promotion" of a point comment to a full position is shown in Figure 10-5.

The form of Marge's position, you will note, is more spectacular and less proper than that of Malone's intervention, but the marking features have a commonality. In both cases, the body is moved as a whole and brought forward. The usual markers of the utterance are exaggerated both in excursion and directness of address.

[3] This drawing is reproduced from *The Stream and Structure of Communicational Behavior, supra.*

Shocking (Marge)   Standing in mock shock (Marge)

FIGURE 10-5.   The exaggeration of an utterance by the use of positional markers

The exaggeration of the forward movement, the face-to-face confrontation, and the stress behavior can also be escalated to a full dominance display. In American males this display looks something as follows: The body is brought into frontal orientation toward the addressee, who is then stared at. If a group is so addressed, the body is brought to an orientation near the center of the group and the face is slowly swept so that each other person is addressed, one at a time. The gaze is directed straight ahead toward the eyes of the addressee, and the eye space is thus commanded.

The body may be brought to its full height. The head, jaw, or chest may be protruded. The voice may be projected loudly or sometimes lowered to a whisper. Sometimes the hands are placed on the hips and sometimes the thumbs are hooked into the pockets or the belt. In extreme cases, a fist may be formed.

The dominance display may be followed by a "parallel schizmogenesis" (Bateson, 1958)—that is, by a matching display of dominance on the part of others present. In such a case, dominance displays may escalate until the group members fight or dissociate. But ordinarily some participant wards off the contest with a display of submissive behavior. Such displays often consist of hunching down, looking down, hiding the hands, cocking the head, smiling, and maybe a conciliatory statement.

Chapter Eleven

The Meta-Transaction

So far, I have tried to illustrate how qualifying acts, complex referencing behavior, and simple instructions and tactics can be introduced into any transaction in order to maintain or change the usual structure of that event. But an entire transaction can be metacommunicational if it is held to prevent or induce change in some larger context. Such transactions are employed to teach, reinforce, or alter the shape of relationships or institutions or even the nature of whole societies. And special kinds of programs have evolved for making such efforts.

In one kind of metacommunicational activity, an attempt is made to alter the behavior and cognitive structure of an individual or a group of people who are unhappy with their lot in life or who are regarded as deviant and difficult. Psychotherapy is an example of this order of correctional procedure.

This chapter describes the usual programming of the psychotherapy sessions. The generalizations here are based on filming, videotaping, or simply observing many hundreds of such sessions in a variety of contexts, in several Western cultures. Of course, any single session is but one phase in a course of psychotherapy; certain changes occur in a course that may not even be presaged in a single session. So I will not do justice in this description of the session to the long-term strategies of psychotherapy, or to the kind of cognitive and behavioral changes that may occur in the procedure.

The Psychotherapy Session

The format does not allow for a symmetrical exchange of similar behavior, as occurs in greeting. Instead, the activity is held on the turf of the servicing agency and follows ground rules established under that institutional aegis. The client presents his problem; the agency representative responds by a ministration, rather than by responding in kind with a presentation of his own.

The psychotherapy session shows some of the programming of a conversation or meeting as well as the features of a servicing procedure. It is thus more complicated and less symmetrical than the greeting, but we can use the same paradigm to describe it. We can say how the frame and the communicational field are established and what shape they usually take, and then we can describe the programming of the dialogue that constitutes the body of the session.

The participants in psychotherapy assemble a frame and set up a communicational field whose properties ordinarily conform to the traditions of psychotherapy and common culture. To do this, they learn and use a set of customary arrangements that have evolved for the occasion. These include a prearranged and furnished place of meeting, a customary set of relationships, a set of ground rules, and an ethos (quality of relatedness and behavior).

A kind of ethos will ordinarily prevail in a session; solemnity and seriousness prevail, as befits the airing of a problem in our culture, but, in any session, some particular affective tone, a particular pace or rhythm, and a degree of involvement are likely to be established. This quality of ethos will probably change during the session, but the change usually represents a fluctuation or a cyclic deviation from a baseline state.

These qualities are not necessarily shared to the same degree by all the participants. The psychotherapist, for example, may school himself not to share a hostile or depressive mood in great intensity in order to keep his "objectivity." On the other hand, he may at least use a display of affectivity that harmonizes with that of the client as a means of fostering rapport. In group or family therapy, people of different attitudes and backgrounds may find it difficult to share a common ethos and synchronize their pace of interaction even when they try. But I am not speaking here of individual emotional reactions to what is said or to life itself, but, instead, of a common tone or quality. These qualities occur as traditional states of ethos in a culture, and certain of them are prescribed for the particular activities and ceremonies of a people.

An affective tone is displayed by the quality of posture and facial set, and as well by the manner of moving and speaking. The participants in a session may share such a state in common from the beginning, but even if they do not, there is a tendency for them to move toward such a commonality as the phase of the session proceeds, for affective tone is not merely a matter of personality. In the tradition of a culture, certain such states are prescribed for given occasions. Solemnity, for example, is expected at a funeral in middle America, and this tone tends to prevail in most psychotherapy sessions. So one exhibits a prescribed tone at least as a matter of etiquette.

Synchrony is established by visible and audible beats (Kendon, 1970; Condon and Ogston, 1966, 1967; Scheflen, 1972). The cadence of language, for instance, is often established for the group by the first speaker of status, though this cadence may be changed a number of times. A beat is also given by the participants in a quite visible way in the nodding of the head or the slow wagging of a leg extended toward the center of the group.

A very visible aspect of the ethos is what Goffman (1971) calls the degree of involvement. Involvement is ordinarily increased by the following dimensions of behavior within the frame: The participants lean closer to each other, uncrossing their arms and then their legs as they do so. They turn toward each other so that they come more and more into a full relation of face to face. They move around less in their seats and reduce the amount of scanning. And often their voices show an increase in affectivity and their faces become more animated.

As we will see, the degree of involvement cyclically increases in a psychotherapy session, ideally attaining a degree that therapists call "rapport." A set of ground rules is established in the field. To some extent, these comply with the usual laws, mores, and etiquette of social class and culture, but courtship and violence are implicitly prohibited, and games of a physical nature are interdicted by the nature of the proceedings. In fact, the featured mode of behavior is language, and the topics of dialogue are to focus upon the life problems of the various group members. If these ground rules are not clear from the outset, the therapist may introduce them by spoken instruction.

The Program of Expositional Activities

The body of the psychotherapy session thus features the exposition of a patient's or a family's problems. This exposition occurs in stages according to an agenda that is quite familiar in America. A problem or a point of view is outlined by a speaker, and this problem is then discussed and explored. Then a disposition or solution is attempted. In psychotherapy sessions, however, this sort of agenda is usually enacted more than once in any given session.

We can picture the succession of events in a session as having three phases—something like a greeting, a conversation, and a parting. An initial, or introductory, period occurs, in which the frame and field are established, after which a number of cycles or rapport and exposition occur; then there is a terminal phase, in which the frame is dissolved and the clients leave.

There is considerable variation in the application of this agenda in an actual session, for sometimes the clients list one problem after another and resist the exploration of any one. Some patients refuse to settle down and present any problem; or sometimes members of a faction spend the entire session arguing about who will talk and what will be recounted. Sometimes a lot of business about appointments or fees or goals will occur at the introductory and terminal periods. But, ordinarily, when the usual programming has been adopted, the initial and terminal phases will occupy but a few minutes, and at least forty minutes of a fifty-minute session will be occupied with cycles of exposition. Thus if there are two cycles, as is usually the case in a classical one-to-one session, each will take about twenty minutes or so to enact. In thirty-minute sessions, cycles of about twelve minutes are usual. Sometimes the cycle is speeded up so that a number of patients can present or the therapist can quickly review the procedure and thus dispose of a number of items of old and familiar business.

But the usual, or classical, segmentation of a session can be diagramed somewhat as follows:

> Introduction: 3 minutes
> Expositional Phase #1:20 minutes
> Expositional Phase #2: 25 minutes
> Termination: 2 minutes

The demarkation of these phases is not an arbitrary matter. The beginning and the ending of each phase are clearly indicated by quite visible behaviors. At the beginning of each phase, the participants will change their bodily posture and thus alter the structure of the subframe, and they will hold this configuration throughout that phase. Then, when the phase is over, the postures will be changed back to the shape of the original frame or else to some other configuration, which will be employed throughout the next phase. In short, the phases of the agenda are marked or punctuated, and thus there is a correspondence between the shape of the subframe and the stream of ideation and speech. We have seen how this process works, in earlier chapters.

If we observe these points of shift and juncture in a psychotherapy session, we will see something as follows: At the beginning of the session, after the people have taken positions, they will mutually engage each other and begin the presentation as a cue from the therapist. He may take the classical posture of listening, direct his eyes and maybe his hand to a particular participant, and ask a leading question, such as, "How have you been?" or "Why don't you tell more about the problem at home?" Then, after the exposition of phase 1, both therapist and client will fall silent, drop their eyes and faces for an instant, and perhaps move back in their chairs to maximum interpersonal distance and cross their arms and/or their legs. Then they will re-engage (move toward each other), and twenty minutes or so later they will perform the behaviors or termination. Then some closing business may be discussed, about appointments or fees or the like, and the participants stand and separate.

Thus shifts of posture and orientation and periods of silence tend to mark phases, but ordinarily some other and special behavior of marking is also used at major points of juncture. Summing up often occurs. Smokers will light up at the beginning of phase 1, at the beginning of phase 2, and often at the end of the session. In one sequence of sessions that we studied, the patient took a sip of water at the end of each phase 1 and each phase 2. In other cases, participants fiddled with their glasses or shoes or rearranged their clothing at juncture points.

We must pay attention to this marking behavior. It occurs in any human transaction we have ever observed. It appears not only in activities that feature speech but in physical tasks, games, and courtships. Some kind of shift in bodily positioning, orientation, and speech flow appears *at all levels of communicational structure* from the gross stages and phases of transaction to the most minute sequencing of words and gestures. Smaller units of movement and speech tend to be marked only by vocal and bodily shifts, but larger phases and changes are marked by changing the over-all frame and by adding special markers.

The traditions of psychotherapy call for an escalation of involvement as the exposition of the problem unfolds. At its maximum degree, this involvement achieves a subjective state of intimacy, trust, mutual interest, and so forth that clinicians and patients call rapport. But the involvement is not supposed to proceed to courtship, and in classical therapies does not include touching or embracing. It is considered a desirable state for exploration and learning, and patients who resist such engagement are taught and encouraged to become involved in rapport.

Mechanically speaking, the escalation to rapport proceeds in a stepwise sequence by an increment of physical closeness, the progressive uncrossing of arms, then legs, and greater face-to-face orientation. The degree of affective display in voice and face also tends to increase with involvement. Then, after a period of about twenty minutes, the involvement is de-escalated as both parties move back to their baseline positions of greater distance and less-direct face-to-face orientation.

As I already suggested, a three-step format of dialogue is employed in each cycle. The client presents a problem; this problem is discussed or explored, and then some kind of tentative suggestion or advice or interpretation is offered. I have also claimed that the escalation of involvement in any cycle also occurs in steps, or increments. Actually the shifts in mode of dialogue and degree of involvement correspond in time. So the agenda of each cycle prescribes a three-step sequence of linguistic activity within an escalation of postural-kinesic shift toward the configuration of rapport.

There is, of course, a good deal of variation from session to session in the employment of this format. The degree of involvement varies greatly, and so does the speed of escalation. The kinds of things a therapist says varies greatly from one school of thought to another. But there is also a variation within a given session between the use of the format in the first and the second phases of the same session. Ordinarily the degree of rapport is greater in the second go-around, and the therapist may make only the briefest comment the first time, whereas he may elaborate his interpretation and suggestions at the last phase of the session and provide time to discuss his ideas with his patient. And in family or group sessions, the participants in the cycle may change with each enactment. Furthermore, the comments of the therapist may be directed to the patient's story, to how he relates the story, or to the way that the involvement itself is managed or avoided. And finally, in consultations or demonstrations to students or in cases of very withdrawn and fearful patients, the escalation may be omitted altogether.

In each step, the participants recount experience, using the communicational code of their culture to do so. For the most part, these representations are limited in subject matter by the rules of psychotherapy and must concern the life problems of the clients or the problems of relationship in the therapy group itself. Usually the representational medium is language and gesture, though in some forms of therapy the clients can present a story in dance or drama form, and in some cases courtship or argument is enacted and rehearsed. But in any event, each step is made up of a succession of still smaller units of representational behavior: positions and point-units (Scheflen, 1964, 1966A, 1966B, 1973).

The Dynamics of Enacting Psychotherapy

The fact that the procedure of psychotherapy is governed by a traditional program does not assure that a session will proceed according to Hoyle. Variations and deviations in fact occur for a variety of reasons; these variations may in turn lead to the institution of regulatory and corrective procedures. But all performances usual or variant in the program of the psychotherapy session are observed, interpreted, and discussed, for tactical and strategic purposes. These matters will not concern us, for I, at best could only touch on this complicated subject. So we had best use the examples to gain a view of communicational process in general rather than as a treatise on the ins and outs of psychotherapy itself.

In any particular session, as we have seen, some number of patients and therapists are present, and these people are of various types. Sometimes the local situation affects the shape of events. In such cases, variations may occur beyond those dictated by the program.

One can imagine, of course, some rather ridiculous or grossly inappropriate circumstances. A patient and a therapist might come together who do not speak the same tongue, for instance, or a violent patient may enter the office and assault the therapist. Or the participants might arrive to find the office in a shambles. Such things do, of course, occur, but they are usually headed off by arrangements such as those described below. More commonly, however, the circumstances do not disrupt the event in any gross way, but they do result in certain variations from the usual program.

Generally, the avoidance of gross mismatching and deviance is managed in systems of territory and social organization that are broader than any session. Psychotherapy is widely prevalent in America and Western Europe, and it appears also in Israel, India, and Japan. In most Western countries, it is a procedure of middle-class and occasionally upper-class people, but it is administered to working-class people in mental hospitals and in recent years in community mental-health clinics. In America, the procedure is largely an activity of WASP, Jewish, and Latin American peoples. Yet people of different linguistic groups do not ordinarily come together in psychotherapy because of territorial boundaries. There are, for example, French psychotherapists for Parisians, psychotherapists of Hispanic culture for the people of Mexico City, and so on. And there are private practitioners of psychotherapy in suburban- or middle-class-urban America for well-to-do Americans and clinics for working-class Americans.

A system of assessment and institutionalization ordinarily routes very deviant and angry clients to hospitals, where they may be seen by hospital therapists. And there are similarly networks and channels for routing clients against whom criminal charges have been filed, and for those with homosexual behavior, problems with alcohol, and so on. Networks of friendship and membership in institutes of psychotherapy also govern the flow of patients of particular types to therapists who are considered to have competence and interest in particular kinds of problems. In short, a system of gates and channels brings patients and therapists of like culture, interest, and lifestyle, together, with some degree of intuitive or informal accuracy.

Once a course of psychotherapy has been contracted, the therapist or his associates undertake a brief course of indoctrination to teach the patient about the program. Often a patient has been briefed on the procedure by a friend or by the hospital or clinic staff before he even sits down to the first session. If not, the psychotherapist may take time at the beginning or the end of the first session to explain what the patient is to do and what the objectives of the procedure are. Then, in subsequent sessions, therapists remind the client of the rules. They initiate the first cycle of rapport and exposition, for example, with a leading question such as, "Tell me more about the problem we discussed last time" or "How have you been feeling since our last session?" In short order, kinesic and vocal cues come to stand for these instructions. For example, a therapist may clear his throat or adopt a certain posture and facial set each time as he instructs the patient to describe a problem. After he has done this a number of times, he has only to clear his throat or adopt the postural-facial set in order to suggest the instructions.

Thus, as Goffman has said (1959), the situation is defined explicitly. But bear in mind that the entire situation instructs about the purposes, agenda, ethos, and quality of the procedure. The type of institutional setting, the room layout, the color scheme and décor, the setting of furniture and dress, the frame, and the use of leading questions and suggestions throughout provide signals about the type of event. A given patient may be quite unacquainted with the details of the psychotherapy program, but he knows *about events of this class*. He knows something, at least, of the usual rules of decorum, dialogue, consultation, assessment, judgment, and syntax.

The behaviors of the psychotherapy session are also regulated and qualified kinesically. Frowning and wiping the index finger across the nostrils is, as usual, a monitor of deviance; picking lint from the clothing occurs at times when an impropriety is confessed; the brows are raised at points of incredulity; and so on. In short, metacommunicative kinesics are used in the meta-transaction as in any other transaction.

Therapists exercise an option in the slot for commentary. The interpretation or advice may be directed to *what* the patient tells or to *how* the patient speaks and acts or to how he relates in rapport. And accordingly the therapist may selectively attend to the patient's historical account, to his recital of problems and symptoms, to his facial sets and voice qualities, or to his quality of involvement. He may also attend to what the patient does *not* say or do.

Now, the therapist has been trained in one or more doctrinal schools that hold theories explaining human delight in developmental or other terms. So the therapist goes through a process of assessing variations and deviations in the patient's behavior. He relates these to a diagnostic or personality type schema, and arrives at an explanation of their origins. Then, at the third step of the cycle, he apprises the patient of some facet of this judgment.

In most schools of psychotherapy, it is considered poor technique to make the interpretation in technical terminology, so therapists rarely say, "You have an unresolved oedipus complex" or "You seem to have a narcissistic oral fixation." They state their assessment instead in rather earthy or everyday language. And in most schools of thought it is considered dangerous or unwise to tell the patient the total interpretation at the outset, so the interpretive comments are usually offered piece by piece over the period of a great many sessions. And generally speaking, the psychotherapist prefers to believe that the patient is discovering these truths for himself rather than being indoctrinated into their acceptance, so he tends to *suggest* interpretive appraisals and to speak of the patient's affirmation of these as an "insight" or "self-realization."

These variations represent but tactics in an over-all strategy that prescribes an appraisal and an acceptance of this appraisal on the part of the patient. The rationale of this strategy holds that people will behave in a more propitious way if they understand the nature and source of deviant thoughts and behavior. This rationale in turn is based on a notion that thoughts and feelings are the cause of behavior.

But psychotherapists do employ the cycles of rapport and exposition in the service of other strategies, and in any session they use certain tactics as ends. One of the most important is an emphasis upon the relationship between therapist and client per se. In classical, insight therapies, this emphasis was focused upon how the patient's incongruent and transcontextual actions toward the therapist arose by the transference of such ways of acting from figures in his early life. In recent years, however, the emphasis has been placed on the quality of relating—on why the patient does not move close, speak intimately, touch, or confront the therapist with anger. And in some cases the patient is actively encouraged to try out and practice such ways of relating.

A third strategy is employed when the client shows behavior that is regarded as an improvement. This behavior is reinforced by operant conditioning. At one extreme, such behavior is simply ignored instead of being subjected to assessment and interpretation. In an intermediate degree of tactical supportiveness, such behavior is praised and encouraged. And, at the other extreme, it is actively reinforced by giving the patient tangible rewards (as in some of the behavioral therapies) or by embracing him when he says the "right" things (as in some encounter and marathon procedures). Therapists differ, however, in their conceptions of such tactics. At one extreme are schools of psychotherapy that ignore all the other strategies I have described, and attribute the entire procedure to the mechanism of operant conditioning. At the other extreme, the psychotherapists deny that conditioning plays a role in the strategies of psychotherapy.

Another strategy seems to play a major role in psychotherapy, particularly in later sessions of a course. A client who has learned or devised a different way of acting tries this out in social relations outside the session. And he fails or succeeds in some measure. He then brings to the expositional slot a description of these experiences for review. The therapist then criticizes the new effort, makes suggestions, and even encourages the patient to practice the newer approaches on him in the session. Then the patient makes a next attempt in his relationships outside the session. In this instance the strategy of psychotherapy is a kind of coaching.

Still other strategies of psychotherapy have been described by Haley (1963); yet, even all these descriptions do not exhaust the repertoire of various psychotherapies. But I have said enough to make the communicational point. Within a classical format for exposition and rapport, a great many uses can be made of the communicational code. Any communicational event shows a variety of tactical and strategic manipulations of the customarily programmed units of behavior.

Comment: On Traditional Meaning

We have now dealt with patterns of representational behavior by which an image of some thing or event can be
mutually conjured. The contexts of this representational activity can specify which of many similar events is being
referred to. In fact, a host of connotations about the event
are specified by the context in which it occurs. Furthermore, additional representational behavior can be added to
qualify or change the meaning of what is being enacted.
These metacommunicational events have a double reference. They are to act upon what is going on at the time,
but in doing so they refer to broad systems of value and
to whole systems of strategies.

We cannot thereby speak of the meaning of any behavior. There is instead a system of meanings in broader
and broader levels of circumstance and experience. Furthermore, we cannot think of any act as having a meaning
of its own, for meaning is not a property of the behavior
itself. The term "meaning" applies instead to a relation
of behavior and context. So when one is asked what a
given behavior means, he must answer as I have tried to
do here, by referring to broader and broader levels of context. He must proceed in some kind of systematic way to
describe the immediate sequencing and framing of the act,
its location in a relationship and in a program on an occasion, and so on. One ultimately ends up by referring to
huge structures such as the institution, the local subculture,
the culture of a whole society, and even to a set of societies
such as Western civilization.

But the contexts that define the meaning of a given act are coded. Certain gestures, emblems, and other representations have come to signify these systems of activity and thought. For instance, a constellation of distance, orientation, and degree of face-to-face closure refers to a whole tradition of relationships and involvements. A single metacommunicative gesture can refer to an entire institutional doctrine, one that has been held in common by the people of a society for many centuries. The quality of speaking, the use of certain words, or the wearing of certain kinds of dress may bring to bear the beliefs and life-styles of an entire rural or urban population in a whole ethnic tradition. So we may have to retrace thousands of years of cultural history, millions of years of species history, and a billion years of evolution to learn how a certain system of coded meanings has come about.

But we cannot understand communication and meaning if we simply recognize an act and say what traditions of thought, value, and behavioral form it brings to mind. We must also ask *why that particular form is appearing at that particular instance.* We must ask what structure is being maintained or changed. We must ask if something is interfering with a traditional pattern of behavior that has evolved to make organisms and environments consonant. We must ask whether that traditional communicational pattern is adequate to the survival of a particular person, group, or society. The tactics, the strategies, and the adaptations of tradition are brought into question whenever a metacommunicational action is observed. In short, to ascertain its meaning, we must know why a behavior is performed.

Any performance carries traditional systems of meaning by its relation to contexts. Yet each traditional behavior is also "loaded" by the addition of paracommunicative features and metacommunicational acts. Thus each communicational action, however small, is coded or "indexed." It carries cues to the states and roles, affiliations and memberships, and the background of the performer. It carries signals about the ideals, values, beliefs, plans, and strategies of its performer. The contexts that specify the meanings of any action are not left to the imagination; they are signaled or indicated. In fact, these contextual references need not be intuitive; they are indicated instead by visible and audible features which we can consciously study.

As a result, we do not have to ask what *the performer* means. In fact, we sometimes prefer not to ask him, for we cannot necessarily trust that he will tell us or that he knows. We can ask instead *how behavior means*. We gain this information from perceiving the structure of behavior— from perceiving the composition of its elements, qualities, and cues in a system of relationships, programs, and situations.

Section Five

The Meaning of Meaning

There is still another dimension of the subject of meaning which we have not yet dealt with in an explicit way. We have approached the point from time to time in this thesis. You may recall, for instance, that we discussed two ways of looking at the paracommunicative features of behavior. One could ask, I pointed out, what a particular style told us about a person or a category of people; one could ask what difference paracommunicational features made in the stream of behavior and experience. And we just touched on the matter when I spoke of asking what behavior means rather than asking what people mean by their behavior. This is an issue of focus: does one focus on people or on behavior forms?

Implied here, however, is a much larger difference in viewpoint. This difference involves total world views: the ways whole societies view human experience. A difference like this transcends cultural boundaries and involves large blocks of society. For instance, it separates Eastern and Western civilization; and it distinguishes classical from post-Einsteinian civilization.

The term "epistemology" is often used to describe a way of looking at nature and experience in general. Naturally the epistemology of a people or of a science will make a great difference in how they view any particular phenomenon, such as human behavior and meaning.

Chapter Twelve

Current Epistemologies in the Study of Behavior

I believe we can make a simple classification of the epistemological views that are currently extant in common culture and science. The classical Western view of people and behavior has two common subforms in American society: the organismic, or individual-centered, and the social, or interreactional, variants.

Approaches to Communication

Consider what I have done in constructing this account. First I reversed the usual priorities in describing a human experience by telling first about the customary programming of behavior in a culture. Then I described variants and additions to the program.

I have not invented this way of looking at communicational events. I have merely illustrated an existing theory and tried to explicate how it is put together. This approach has evolved since the social-science and behavioral-science era of the 1950s. It is sometimes called "human communication theory," and a variety of theorists and researchers have contributed to it, including Birdwhistell (1952, 1960, 1961, 1966); Bateson (1955, 1972); Goffman (1959, 1961, 1963); Scheflen (1963, 1964, 1965, 1966A, 1966B, 1967, 1972, 1973A); Kendon (1967, 1970, 1972); Kendon and Ferber (1973); Beels, Ferber, and Schoonbeck (1973), and a great many others. This approach is based upon structural studies of communicational behavior by a method known as context analysis (McQuown et al., 1971; Scheflen, 1966B). It is similar to the approaches of structural linguistics (Sapir, 1921; Bloomfield, 1933; Pike, 1954; Hockett, 1958) and to studies done in the more recent tradition of patterns of culture (Benedict, 1946; Mead, 1951), for it evolved from these. And the methodology is quite like that which is used by the ethologists (Schneirla, 1951; Lorenz, 1952; McBride, 1964).

Notice, however, that it differs from the sociological approaches to communication and communicational networks and to psychological studies of a structural kind, in that it begins with a focus on cultural forms of behavior instead of upon groups or people who behave. These approaches need not be irreconcilable. One can start with a description of traditional forms and move on to how these are employed by people, as I have done. Or one can begin with groups of people and move to a picture of the behavioral structures they evolve and use. The important notion that underlies the study in either case is a structural view; it is this I want to describe now in evolutionary terms, for both structural and systems research have emerged in this century as part of an extensive epistemological revolution. Thus they differ markedly in method and model from classical, Aristotelian views.

This idea of behavioral structure and of a communicational field approximates the view that Einstein recommended (Einstein, 1920). He used this approach to solve the Newtonian problem of gravity and ether. The problem was this: The Newtonians had focused on the physical bodies in space, and, using a billiard-ball model, they had concentrated on two bodies such as earth and sun and asked how these masses interacted. Since no action could be seen, one was postulated and called gravity. But now the classical physicists dug themselves even farther into a conceptual hole. To explain this action-at-a-distance, they posited that a substance of some kind existed between the bodies in space. This substance was subsequently named "ether." It was then classified by types, and treated from then on as an actuality of some kind or other.

Einstein approached the problem in a very different way. He did not narrow his observational focus to some bodies but attended to all of them, and he did not concentrate on the bodies themselves but on their arrangement. He then conceived of their arrangement and pattern of motion as a function of a large field, i.e., of the interdependency of speed and mass. He did not see the bodies as the cause of the action of gravity, nor did he see them as emitting any force. In fact, he explicitly warned us not to look at the matter this way. The bodies in space moved in ordered ways. They did not act on each other.

Consider that we have had almost the same conceptual problem in the sciences of man until at least about 1955. We looked at participants in a relationship or a communicational event and perceived that their behavior was interrelated, so we assumed that they influenced each other. And we then postulated that some force operated between them. We drew a line between them on a box-and-line diagram to show a relationship, and then we abstracted this relationship as transmission or communication or interaction or something of the kind. And when we broke down this idea into its constituents, we usually imagined a force of some kind emanating from each participant. We called this force emission or emergence or emotion or energy or expression or something of the kind. And we located the origins of this action within the participants, calling it a motive or need or drive or intent or emotion or instinct or whatever.

Then we assumed that these imaginary forces were the cause of the phenomena we observed. In an expression theory of communication, we believed that the behavior of each person was an emergence of his thoughts or motives or instincts. In an interaction theory, we simplistically regarded one person's behavior as the cause of the other's behavior, and vice versa. So we saw only part of the situation and thus got lost in first-cause, or essence, or real-truth dogmas about communication and behavior. These are useful for political activities such as concealing how things work or shifting blame, but they do not do anything for science. And each part-truth leaves room for another dogma about the element that was omitted from consideration, so we end up with multiple, warring doctrinal schools.

Each of these practices is traditional, of course, in Western thought and Aristotelian logic.[1] All of us grow up believing that the universe consists of forms or things (represented by nouns) and of actions (represented by verbs). And the structure of our language dictates that we look first at things and then state what these things do. In fact, we Westerners take actions and forces for granted to the degree that we postulate them even when we cannot see them or demonstrate their existence. We make up conceptions to account for action and then come to regard these conceptions as things or forces in themselves. Then we take another step in imagination: we regard the explanations (which we now see as forces in things and people) as the causes of the phenomena we see. So we fall into a circular mode in which we think our explanations cause the things we are explaining. So we end up with ideas of unknowables that only an "expert" can "see."

If you think back in the history of science, you will remember that Einstein was only one of the people who introduced constraints of this kind at the turn of the twentieth century. Similar ways of looking at phenomena were used in quantum theory and the thermodynamics of that era, and appeared in continental-drift theory, for instance. And the idea was put forth at that time by Cannon (1920), who described homeostasis in living systems, and by the *Gestalt* theorists in describing perception. Freud's description of cognitive processes in the analysis of the dream (S. Freud, 1913) was a concept of this kind. So was Tolman's idea of cognitive maps (Tolman, 1932). And the ideas of culture in general (Malinowski, 1913) and of the structural unit of language (Sapir, 1921; Bloomfield, 1933)

[1] I am here using the term "Aristotelian" in the following senses: first, that some real truth, or prime cause, or essence is invoked to explain a phenomenon, and accordingly that reductionistic approaches are used in definition and research; and second, that a dichotomy is made between things and actions, and the actions tend to be imaged as forces that emerge from the things. In a way, then, I am setting up Aristotelian thought as a straw man to contrast with systems thinking.

were of this type, though these constructs developed a decade or two later.

These approaches had certain features in common. The observational focus was upon fields, or groups of events that bore a relation to each other and thus formed a configuration. These elements or changes or behaviors were not seen as acting on each other or as causing each other in any direct way. And each change in a linear direction was seen as but one element of the field or group, being associated with other changes which collectively held some kind of steady-state or unit form. Methodologically speaking, each of these views was achieved by a structural approach to research. In this approach a researcher analyzes a whole, or unit, to identify its component elements, but he is not permitted to single out one of these as a basis for explaining the whole. He must instead turn in an integrative direction and examine the relations between elements to see how they are assembled or patterned in the formation of the whole.

These early approaches, however, fell short in an important way. They were used locally, so to speak, to describe but a single unit of activity among the multiple interrelated systems of activity. Thus the physiologists applied homeostasis only to activities within the organism, and the psychologists stuck to questions of perception, or cognition. And the structural linguists refused to attend to either discourse or to meaning.

As a consequence, little attention was paid within any discipline to the contexts in which some particular event unit or structure appeared. Thus the physiologists studied suborganismic systems in great detail, but they usually were content to merely represent environment with arrows and to speak of it as though it consisted of simple changes in the weather or of gross dangers or toxins. They did not see the environment of man as complexly structured by territorial arrangements, built environments, and patterns of culture. Similarly the learning theorists such as Pavlov (1927) and Thorndike (1911) were content to represent the stimulus as a simple vector. In fact, society, culture, economics, and the like were usually but names to be placed in a circle at the other end of a stimulus arrow and listed as "environmental determinants." And the response, too, was usually represented as a simple arrow of emission or output, so the psychologists did not bother to describe the structure of the behaviors with which they worked. Freud did describe the contexts of his patients' early learning experience in order to account for their persistent patterns of acting (S. Freud, 1905), but he became more abstract as the twentieth century wore on, and his followers rarely bothered to describe contexts at all. They instead reduced behaviors to abstract ideas that all too often conveyed images of energy and force.

In short, the early structural theories did not follow Einstein's lead and describe a field or event unit as a function of larger and larger contexts. Instead, they merely returned to the old, Aristotelian practice of representing a context as a simple vector of input or output. Thus we again got lost in the business of forces and causes.

This state of provincial focus prevailed in the science of man until the 1950s, when extensive interest in social and then in cultural phenomena developed in common culture and in all the sciences of man, including the traditionally organismic sciences of biology, medicine, psychology, and psychiatry. At this time, interests in the relation of behaviors among and between people and theories, interaction, and communication, were developed. The conceptual root of these constructs appears to go back to the 1940s, when cybernetics explicated the concept of feedback (McCulloch, 1949; Wiener, 1948) and information (Shannon and Weaver, 1949), and general systems theory (Bertalanffy, 1950, 1960) emerged. The concept of retroaction forces us to examine the contexts of an event, for the mechanisms cannot be found in a phenomenon itself, but appear instead at higher levels of organization. By the same token, the concept of retroaction allows us to synthesize a picture of complex, simultaneous relations that does not emerge if we use a linear model of causation.

In short, then, we have moved in this century from a

things-and-forces view to a view of structures or fields within which certain organizations of activity are maintained. This view has been slow of adoption when it comes to looking at man himself, maybe because it displaces him from his imaginary position of central causation and control. In any event, we do not now see people as the cause of communication. Instead we place people in communicational fields and networks. We see them as activating, changing, and manipulating these fields, but not as causing them.

Using and Extending a Systems Approach

My preference for a structural and systems approach to the study of human behavior is based on the opportunity this epistemology provides for building a science of knowables and observables. But surely you will say I must agree that an Aristotelian view has certain uses—you will remind me that a Newtonian physics is still important to study certain physical phenomena even though it has been supplanted by an Einsteinian approach in astronomy.

I readily agree that an organismic view is useful for studying individual people and organisms, and that a classical social approach is useful to define the membership of groups and social organization. I agree that classical methods are important in studying the mechanisms of metabolism, physiology, and psychological processes. An approach that focuses upon the motives, traits, and personality features of individuals is tactically important in corrective and disciplinary procedures. But even here I have some reservations. I believe that the organism-centered approach is considerably and dangerously misused. We cannot discuss the physiological and psychological behaviors of people without respect to their adaptations in communicational systems and without respect to the institutional and cultural behaviors they have learned in becoming people. Yet many of the organismic sciences have done this in the past. In addition, we do not want to remain hung up on linear causation theories which hold that human behavior is determined by personality or motive alone. Above all, we must

avoid a simplistic notion that certain people or factions are
the cause of social events and problems. In this case the
organismic approach is used politically—to blame, label,
and scapegoat. This process not only results in injustice
but keeps us from understanding social problems in a more
holistic way.

So even though I was trained as a physician, as a neuro-
scientist, and then as a psychoanalyst, I have come to prefer a structural and behavioral view as a starting place for
the study of human behavior and experience. I would, however, like to develop and extend this view so that it takes
more account of individual differences and suborganismic
events such as cognition, neural processes, and, ultimately,
metabolic processes. I have done this in a limited way by
discussing paracommunicational issues and pointing out
that the metacommunicational behavior of participants indicates their values, beliefs, and strategies. But we have
hardly scratched the surface in building a systems view of
behavioral integration at all levels of organization. To do
so we will have to at least take cognizance of some processes of the kind I will now mention.

Consider first the organismic processes that must be involved in a communicational situation when a degree of
commonality and accord is achieved.

First, people occupy places, establish a formation of
postural-orientational relations, and in some measure share
a speed and rhythm of movement, a feeling tone or ethos,
and images of a common system of representations.

To do this, a common state of perceptual *Gestalten,* a
common state of neuronal fields (Sherrington, 1948), and
a similar level of autonomic, hormonal, and metabolic
states must be established. This results in a dynamic equilibrium.

A number of contextual features allow this possibility.
The human organisms meet in a stable environmental setting and achieve a common state of ecosystems equilibrium. We must assume that such states are consonant with
genetically coded physiological states, but that these have
also been learned in common in larger systems of kinship,

institutional membership, and common culture. The particular state of a communicational field seems to be indicated or signaled by customary arrangements of schedule and occasion, by the arrangements and decoration of places and participants, by the shape of groups and frames, and by facial and postural configurations. When such an equilibrium is achieved, it is rapidly habituated and the participants apparently do not have to be conscious of its behavioral elements.

Such states change from time to time in the programmatic sequences of transaction. Each of these steps or stages may be familiar to the participants, so they know when a phase has been completed, but a system of shifts and markers also signals a next step, and a recalibration of states and relations is thereby required.

But there are times when participants do not share the pace and ethos of a phase or perform the expected parts in the program. And sometimes there are ambiguity and uncertainty about what is to come next. At such times the participants scan the scene and look for cues. A flurry of cues, signals, or instructions are then enacted.

So we must account for the fact that participants change their states and relations from time to time. The markers and the behaviors of search seem to be signs of a change of this type. Their appearance elicits an orienting reflex (Sokolov, 1960). This reflex, in turn, must be followed by the experience of a new perceptual *Gestalt*. And a set of retroactive physiological mechanisms must be triggered to a set in a new state of equilibrium.

Pribram (1971) postulates that biased homeostats[2] continuously monitor blood sugar, oxygen level, and the like. These systems regulate metabolic states within certain limits, but information about these states is transmitted to subcortical and cortical centers. These inputs of information can be matched with images of the program in process

[2] A biased homeostat is a regulatory mechanism, in this case a neural mechanism that monitors a metabolic state. If a level of oxygen, blood glucose, or the like rises above or falls below a certain pre-established level, a retroactive, or feedback, loop will correct this deviation from normal level.

and with plans for carrying it out (Miller, Galanter, and Pribram, 1960). And these are in turn matched with an ongoing perception of the behaviors of the participants (including one's own). Such mechanisms are described in detail by Pribram (1971).

Changes in state and context are apparently experienced by participants as emotions. More-conscious images of the structure of the activity can also be elicited by change and matched to an image of the usual standards, values, and explanations of the procedure. These may be verbalized as metacommunicative statements or merely thought without motor enactment. These representations and affective states are visibly indicated whenever the ongoing events are not congruent with customary images, plans, and standards. In such cases, thoughts and feelings appear to be simultaneous or *post hoc* commentaries on the ongoing events. But when these are followed by metacommunicative actions, a corrective mechanism is introduced. But in neither case should we view thoughts and feelings as a simple cause of the programmatic behaviors of the communicational event.

People react to changes in state and to incongruities, and their actions tend to restore more-usual states of relation, affect, and order. People thus act as complex biased homeostats in a social network for maintaining the existing social order (Scheflen, 1972). Affective states and a preoccupation with metarepresentations can last, of course, long beyond the terminals of any given transaction. In fact they can become lifelong characteristics of a family or a person. In this case we may abstract them as personality traits and find that they influence the kinds of communicational events and role that a participant finds himself engaged in. So retroactive (feedback) loops involving judgment, value, and heightened affective states play an important role in human behavior. Some people thus become the bearers of stasis at the social level.

We should also bear in mind that all the recalibrations in organismic state and behavior that we observe in a communication are not mere reactions to the ongoing course of audible and visible events. The failure to eat, for example, or a falling room temperature may evoke motor responses that alter or even disrupt the enactment of a program. Furthermore, people do not necessarily confine their activities to the enactment of conventional parts. In behaving transcontextually, participants bring into an event elements of behavior that ordinarily belong to some other kind of activity. They may use these elements to establish new relationships, change the program of activities to another kind, and in other ways manipulate the situation or return it to the *status quo.*

It is evident, then, that people carry multiple, simultaneous images of the procedures of their culture and can enact programs not called for by the immediate setting and occasion. And recombinations of familiar programs are used to deal with special conditions so that cultural differences can be bridged and changing conditions dealt with.

In this latter case, quite conscious behavioral integrations are interposed in the retroactive and (feedforward) loops of the communicational process. So we can regard thoughts as a determinant of communicational behavior, at least when transcontextual or innovative activities are carried out.

In summary, I postulate that at least four successive neurobehavioral mechanisms of greater and greater complexity are mediated by human organisms. Maybe each of these appeared in some successive stage of evolution. (1) In the simplest case, a system of frames, ties, and states are shared in common in response to some prevailing environmental condition. (2) Within this frame, a set of customary and automatic activities are carried out. But some of these are representations of distant things and experiences, so they require the ability to behave symbolically. (3) In cases of ambiguity or incongruity, a set of metacommunicative and recalibration processes take place. These must be based upon an ability to represent standards and values and to compare similar forms of activity. (4) And certain purposive manipulative procedures can be introduced into any enactment so that the forms of communicational behavior can be used for various practical and strategic purposes.

Some Relations of Communicational Events to Social Contexts

The long-range contexts of such events appear in systems of cultural and genetic transmission, but a communicational event also takes place within a social organization. Plans for manipulation, for example, have reference to social hierarchies, career ladders, institutional goals, and so forth. And the participants at a scene may behave in certain ways because of commitments to a faction they represent or in order to maintain ties with affiliates or organizations not actually present. The composition of the group itself is determined by mechanisms of social relationship and the necessity of completing certain activities within various institutions such as the family and the corporation.

With ideals like these we can extend our views of human behavior to levels below that of individual parts and roles to the processes of organ systems, neuronal and other cellular behavior, and so on. But I think we must extend our grasp of the phenomena of human communication in social contexts as well.

In a harmonious and stable case, we may find that systems at all levels of organization are in dynamic equilibrium. Thus, metabolic and social systems are interrelated, and programs of activity can maintain a stable and adaptive relationship between organisms and environments. But institutional and social programs are in many ways obsolete. They do not necessarily evolve fast enough to meet population explosions and other changes. So we must evolve new communicational programs and new institutions. We need to know more about these processes.

Furthermore, the development of a unified and single context is often impossible and not necessarily desirable. I think we need fewer ethnocentric judgments in our internal affairs and less homogeneity of our world populations. We need higher variance, and programs of behavior that tolerate non-agreement and multiple definitions of a situation. I wish we knew more about how these are attained.

Comment: Meaning
in
Different
Epistemologies

These epistemologies are each in common usage, so we can view meaning itself in one of several lights. For instance, we can view problems in human communication in a sort of pre-Copernican way, as is commonplace in the Protestant ethic and in contemporary middle-class America. In this mode, we stress how different we all are, and how high individuality is in some measure inimical to communicational participation. So a current view fosters more human interaction. We can also falter over our innovative natures and our ingenious ability to control nature and our own destinies. But such ideas may be reassuring in a false sense, for they may keep us from exploring the structure of traditional institutional and cultural constraints. It is important to remember that the epistemology we employ in approaching any event will make a great difference in the kinds of answers and meanings we deduce.

Bibliography

Abraham, K.   *Selected Papers on Psychoanalysis.* London:
                 Hogarth, 1949.

Altmann, S. A.   *Social Communication Among Primates.* Chi-
                 cago: Univ. of Chicago Press, 1967.

Austin, W. M.   Personal communication, 1962.

Bales, R. F.   *Interaction Process Analysis.* Cambridge, Mass.:
                 Addison-Wesley, 1950.

Barker, R. G.   *The Stream of Behavior.* New York: Appleton,
                 1963.

Bastain, J.   "Primate signaling systems and human lan-
                 guages." In DeVore, I. (ed.). *Primate Behavior.*
                 New York: Holt, 1965.

Bateson, G.   "The Message. 'This Is Play.'" In Schaffner, B.
                 (ed.). *Group Processes.* Vol. II. New York:
                 Macy, 1955.

———.   *Naven.* Stanford, Calif.: Stanford Univ. Press
                 (2nd ed.), 1958.

———.   Chapter 1. In McQuown, N. (ed.): *The Natural
                 History of an Interview.* In microfilm. Library
                 of Univ. of Chicago, 1971.

———.   *Steps to an Ecology of Mind.* San Francisco:
                 Chandler, 1972.

Beels, C. C.,   *Context Analysis of a Family Interview.* Dem-
Ferber, J. S.,   onstration movie and article (in press) 1973.
and Schoon-
beck, J. A.

Benedict, R.   *Patterns of Culture.* New York: Mentor, 1946.

Berger, M. M.   "Nonverbal Communications in Group Psychotherapy," *Int'l J. Group Psychother.* 8:161–78 (Apr.) 1958.

Bertalanffy, L. von.   "An Outline of General Systems Theory," *Brit. J. Phil. Sci.* 1:134, 1950.

——.   *Problems of Life.* New York: Harper, 1960.

Birdwhistell, R. L.   *Introduction to Kinesics.* Louisville, Ky.: Univ. of Louisville Press, 1952.

——.   "Contribution of Linguistic-Kinesic Studies to the Understanding of Schizophrenia." In Auerback, A. (ed.): *Schizophrenia.* New York: Ronald, 1959.

——.   "Kinesics and Communication." In Carpenter, E. and McLuhan, M. (eds.): *Explorations in Communication.* Boston: Beacon, 1960.

——.   "Paralanguage: 25 years after Sapir." In Brosin, H. (ed.). *Lectures on Experimental Psychiatry.* Pittsburgh: Univ. of Pittsburgh Press, 1961.

——.   "An Approach to Communication," *Family Process* I:194–201 (Sept.) 1962.

——.   Personal Communication. 1963.

——.   Personal Communication. 1964.

——.   "Some Relations Between American Kinesics and Spoken American English." In Smith, A. G. (ed.). *Communication and Culture.* New York: Holt, 1966.

——.   Personal Communication. 1967.

——.   "Communication Without Words." In Alexandre, P. (ed.): *L'Aventure Humaine.* Encyclopédie des Sciences de l'Homme, pp. 157–66. Paris: Kister, S.A., 1968.

——.   Chapter 3. In McQuown, N. (ed.): *The Natural History of an Interview.* Microfilm. Library of Univ. of Chicago, 1971A.

——.   *Kinesics and Context.* Philadelphia: Univ. of Pennsylvania Press, 1971B.

Bloomfield, L.   *Language.* New York: Holt, 1933.

Brosin, H.   In McQuown, N. A. et al.: *The Natural History of an Interview.* Microfilm. Library of Univ. of Chicago, 1971.

Bullowa, M., "The Acquisition of a Word," *Language and*
Jones, L. G., *Speech* 7:107–11, April 1964.
and
Duckert, A. R.

Cannon, W. B. *Bodily Changes in Pain, Hunger, Fear and Rage* (2nd ed.), New York: Appleton, 1920.

Carnap, R. *Meaning and Necessity.* Chicago: Univ. of Chicago Press, 1947.

Charney, E. J. "Postural Configurations in Psychotherapy," *Psychosomatic Medicine* 28 (July 1966): 305–15.

Cherry, C. *On Human Communication.* New York: Science Editions, 1962.

Colby, K. M. *An Introduction to Psychoanalytic Research.* New York: Basic Books, 1960.

Condon, "Sound Film Analysis of Normal and Patho-
W. S. & logical Behavior Patterns," *J. Nerv. & Ment.*
Ogston, W. D. *Dis.* 143:338–47. 1966.

———. "A segmentation of behavior," *J. Psychiat. Research* 5:221–35 (Nov.) 1967.

Darwin, C. *The Expression of the Emotions in Man and Animals.* New York: Philosophical Library, 1955.

Davis, M. A. "Movement Characteristics of Hospitalized Psychotic Patients," *Proceedings of Fifth Annual Conference of the American Dance Therapy Association.* New York, 1970 (available from ADTA, 5173 Phantom Court, Columbia, Md. 21043).

DeVore, I. *Primate Behavior.* New York: Holt, 1965.
(ed.).

Diamond, *The Waste Collectors.* New York: Columbia
S. G., and Univ. Dept. of Anthropology paper, 1966.
Schein, M. D.

Diebold, A. R. "Anthropology and the Comparative Psychology of Communicative Behavior." In Sebeok, T. A. (ed.). *Animal Communication.* Bloomington: Indiana Univ. Press, 1968.

Efron, D. *Gesture and Environment.* New York: King's Crown, 1941.

Eibl- "The Interaction of Unlearned Behavior Pat-
Eibesfeldt, I. terns and Hearing in Mammals." In Delafres-
naye, J. F. (ed.). *Brain Mechanisms and Learning.* Oxford, England: Blackwell Scientific Publications, 1961.

——. "Transcultural Patterns of Ritualized Contact Behavior." In Esser, A. H. (ed.). *Behavior and Environment: The Use of Space by Animals and Men.* New York: Plenum Press, 1971.

Einstein, A. *Relativity; the Special and General Theory.* New York: Holt, 1920.

Ekman, P. "Differential Communication by Head and Body Cues," *J. Personality & Soc. Psychol.* 2:725–35, 1965.

Ekman, P. and "Nonverbal Behavior in Psychotherapy Re-
Friesen, search." In Schlien, J. (ed.). *Research on Psy-
W. V. chotherapy.* Vol. III. Washington, D.C.: American Psychological Assoc., 1968.

——. "The Repertoire of Non-Verbal Behavior: Categories, Origins, Usage and Coding," *Semiotica* 1:49–98, 1969.

Eldred, S. H. "A Linguistic Evaluation of Feeling States in
and Psychotherapy," *Psychiatry* 21:115–21, 1958.
Price, D. B.

Erikson, K. *Wayward Puritans: A Study in the Sociology of Deviance.* New York: Wiley, 1966.

Exline, R. V. "Explorations in the Process of Person Perception," *J. Personality* 31:1–20 (Mar.) 1963.

Exline, R. V. "Affective Relations and Mutual Glances in
and Dyads." In Tomkins, S. S. and Izard, C. E.
Winters, (eds.). *Affect, Cognition, and Personality.* New
L. C. York: Springer, 1965.

Frank, L. K. "Tactile Communication," *Genetic Psychology Monographs* 56:209–55, 1957.

Freud, A. *The Ego and the Mechanisms of Defense.* New York: Int'l Univs. Press, 1946.

Freud, S. *The Interpretation of Dreams.* New York: Macmillan, 1913.

——. "Fragment of an Analysis of a Case of Hysteria." Collected Papers, Vol. III. London: Hogarth, 1950.

——. *Psychopathology of Everyday Life.* New York. In The American Library, 1959.

Gleason, H. A.   *An Introduction to Descriptive Linguistics.* New York: Holt, 1955.

Goffman, E.   *The Presentation of Self in Everyday Life.* Garden City, N.Y.: Doubleday, 1959.

——.   *Asylums.* Garden City, N.Y.: Doubleday, 1961A.

——.   *Encounters.* Indianapolis: Bobbs-Merrill, 1961B.

——.   *Behavior in Public Places.* Glencoe, Ill.: Free Press, 1963.

——.   *Relations in Public.* New York: Basic Books, 1971.

Gottschalk, L. A. (ed.).   *Comparative Psycholinguistic Analysis of Two Psychotherapeutic Interviews.* New York: Int'l Univs. Press, 1961.

Haley, J.   *Strategies of Psychotherapy.* New York: Grune, 1963.

Hall, E. T.   "A System for the Rotation of Proxemic Behavior," *Amer. Anthropol.* 65:1003–26, 1963.

Harris, M.   *The Nature of Cultural Things.* New York: Random House, 1964.

Harris, Z.   *Methods in Structural Linguistics.* Chicago: Univ. of Chicago Press, 1951.

——.   "Discourse Analysis," *Language* 28:1, 1952.

Hewes, G. W.   "World Distribution of Certain Postural Habits," *American Anthropologist* 57:231–44, 1955.

Hockett, C. F.   *A Course in Modern Linguistics.* New York: Macmillan, 1958.

Hockett, C. F. and Ascher, R.   "The Human Revolution," *Current Anthropology* 5:135–67 (June) 1964.

Jaffe, J.   "Language of the Dyad," *Psychiatry* 21:249, 1958.

Joos, M.   "Description of Language Design," *J. Acoust. Soc. Amer.* 22:701–8 (Nov.) 1950.

Kaufman, I. C. and Rosen-blum, L. A. "A Behavioral Taxonomy for *Macaca Nemestrina* and *Macaca Radiata*," *Primates* 7:205–58, 1966.

Kendon, A. "Some Functions of Gaze Direction in Social Interaction," *Acta Psychologica* 26:22–63, 1967.

———. Personal communication, 1969.

———. "Movement Coordination in Social Interaction," *Acta Psychologica* 32:100–25, 1970.

———. "Some Relationships Between Body Motion and Speech." In Siegman, A. W. and Pope, B. (eds.). *Studies in Dyadic Communication*. Elmsford, N.Y.: Pergamon, 1972.

Kendon, A. and Ferber, A. "A Description of Some Behavior Greetings." In Michael, R. P. and Cook, J. H. (eds.). *Comparative Ecology and the Behavior of Primates*. London: Academic Press, 1973.

Korzybski, A. *Science and Sanity*. Lakeville, Conn.: International Non-Aristotelian Library, 1948.

Lancaster, J. B. "Object naming and the emergence of language." In DeVore, P. L. (ed.): *The Origins of Man*. New York: The Wenner-Gren Foundation, 1965.

Lenneberg, E. H. *The Biological Foundations of Language*. New York: Wiley, 1967.

Lévi-Strauss, C. *Structural Anthropology*. New York: Basic Books, 1963.

Lewin, K. *Field Theory in Social Science*. New York: Harper, 1951.

Lorenz, K. *King Solomon's Ring*. New York: Crowell, 1952.

McBride, G. *A General Theory of Social Organization and Behavior*. St. Lucia, Que.: Queensland University Press, 1964.

———. *1966 Seminars at the Center for Advanced Studies in the Behavioral Sciences*. Stanford, Calif., 1966 (unpublished).

———. "On the Evolution of Human Language," *Social Science Information* 7: 81–85, 1968.

McCulloch, W. S. "The Brain As a Computing Machine," *Electronic Eng.* June 1949.

McQuown, N. A., et al.   *The Natural History of the Interview.* Microfilm. Library of University of Chicago, 1971.

Mahl, G. F.   "Gestures and Body Movements in Interviews." In Schlien, J. (ed.). *Research on Psychotherapy.* Vol. III. Washington, D.C.: American Psychological Assoc., 1968.

Mead, M.   "Columbia University Research in Contemporary Cultures." In H. Guetzkow (ed.). *Groups, Leadership and Men.* Pittsburgh: Carnegie Press, 1951.

Menninger, K.   *Theory of Psychoanalytic Technique.* New York: Basic Books, 1958.

Miller, G. A., Galanter, E., and Pribram, K. H.   *Plans and the Structure of Behavior.* New York: Holt, 1960.

Morris, C. W.   *Signs, Language and Behavior.* New York: Prentice-Hall, 1946.

Mowrer, O. H.   "The Psychologist Looks at Language," *Amer. Psychol.* 9:660–94, 1954.

Osgood, C. E.   "On Understanding and Creating Sentences," *Amer. Psychol.* 18:735–52 (Dec.) 1963.

Osgood, C. E. and Sebeok, T. A. (eds.).   "Psycho-Linguistics: A Survey of Theory and Research Problems," *Intl. J. Amer. Linguistics.* Memoir 10. 1964.

Parsons, T.   "Introduction." In Parsons, T. et al. (eds.). *Theories of Society.* Vol. I. Glencoe, Ill.: Free Press, 1961.

Pavlov, I. P.   *Conditioned Reflexes.* London: Oxford University Press, 1927.

Pike, K. L.   *Language. Part I.* Glendale, Calif.: Summer Institute of Linguistics, 1954.

———.   "Toward a Theory of Structure of Human Behavior," *General Systems* 2:135–41, 1957.

Pittenger, R. E., Hockett, C. F., and Danehy, J. J.   *The First Five Minutes.* Ithaca, N.Y.: Paul Martineau, 1960.

Pittenger,   "A Basis for Some Contributions of Linguistics
R. E., and   to Psychiatry," *Psychiatry* 20:1, (Feb.) 1957.
Smith, H. L.,
Jr.

Pribram,   "Toward a Science of Neuropsychology." In
K. H. \   *Current Trends in Psychology and the Be-
                havioral Sciences*. Pittsburgh: University of
                Pittsburgh Press, 1955.

———.   *Languages of the Brain*. Englewood Cliffs, N.J.:
                Prentice-Hall, 1971.

Redfield,   *Levels of Integration in Biological and Social
R. (ed.).   Systems*. Biological Symposia 8. Lancaster, Pa.:
                Cattell, 1942 (pp. 1–240).

Rotter, J. B.   *Social Learning and Clinical Psychology*. Engle-
                wood Cliffs, N.J.: Prentice-Hall, 1954.

Ruesch, J. and *Communication: The Social Matrix of Psychi-
Bateson, G.   atry*. New York: Norton, 1951.

Sapir, E.   *Language*. New York: Harcourt, 1921.

———.   "Speech as a Personality Trait." In D. G. Man-
                delbaum (ed.). *Selected Writings [of Edward
                Sapir] in Language, Culture, and Personality*.
                Berkeley: Univ. of Calif. Press, 1949.

Schaeffer,   *Videotape Techniques in Anthropology*. Doc-
J. H.   toral Thesis, Dept. of Anthropology, Columbia
                Univ., 1970 (unpublished).

Saussere,   *Cours de linguistique générale*. Paris, Bally &
F. de.   Sachdraye, 1949.

Scheflen, A. E. *A Psychotherapy of Schizophrenia*. Springfield,
                Ill.: Thomas, 1961.

———.   "Communication and Regulation in Psychother-
                apy," *Psychiatry* 26:126 (May) 1963.

———.   "The Significance of Posture in Communication
                Systems," *Psychiatry* 27:316–31 (Nov.) 1964.

———.   "Quasi-Courting Behavior in Psychotherapy,"
                Psychiatry 28:245–57 (Aug.) 1965.

———.   "Natural History Method in Psychotherapy:
                Communication Research." In Gottschalk, L. A.
                and Auerbach, A. H. (eds.). *Methods of Re-
                search in Psychotherapy*. New York: Appleton,
                1966A.

———. *Stream and Structure of Communicational Behavior.* Behavioral Monogr. #1, Commonwealth of Penna., 1966B.

———. "On the Structuring of Human Communication," *Amer. Behav. Scientist* 10:8–12 (Apr.) 1967.

———. "Human Communication: Behavioral Programs and Their Integration in Interaction," *Amer. Behav. Scientist* 13:44–55 (Jan.) 1968.

———. "Templates, Blueprints and Programs on Human Behavior." In Grey, Duhl, and Rizzo (eds.). *General Systems Theory and Psychiatry.* Boston: Little, Brown, 1969.

———. *Communicational Structure: Analysis of a Psychotherapy Transaction.* Bloomington, Ind.: Indiana Univ. Press, 1973.

Scheflen, A. E., Kendon, A., and Schaeffer, J. "Audiovisual Media in Research." In Berger, M. (ed.). *Videotape Techniques in Psychiatric Training and Treatment.* New York: Brunner/Mazel, 1970.

Scheflen, A. E. and Scheflen, A. *Body Language and the Social Order.* Englewood Cliffs, N.J.: Prentice-Hall, 1972.

Schneirla, T. C. "Levels in the Psychological Capacities of Animals." In Sellars, R. W., et al. (eds.). *Philosophy for the Future.* New York: Macmillan, 1949.

———. "The Levels Concept in the Study of Social Organization in Animals." In Rohrer, J. H. and Sherif, M. (eds.). *Social Psychology at the Crossroads.* New York: Harper, 1951.

Shannon, C. E. and Weaver, W. *The Mathematical Theory of Communication.* Urbana: Univ. of Ill. Press, 1949.

Sherrington, C. *The Integrative Action of the Nervous System.* New Haven: Yale Univ. Press, 1948.

Simpson, G. G. "The Status of the Study of Organisms," *Amer. Scientist* (March) 1962.

Sokolov, E. N. "Neuronal Models and the Orienting Reflex." In Brazier, M. A. B. (ed.). *The Central Nervous System and Behavior.* Third Conference. New York: Macy, 1960 (pp. 187–276).

Thorndike,   *Animal Intelligence.* New York: Macmillan,
E. L.   1911.

Thorpe, W. H.   *Learning and Instinct in Animals.* Cambridge,
                  Mass.: Harvard Univ. Press, 1956.

Tolman, E. C.   *Purposive Behavior in Animals and Men.* New
                  York: Century, 1932.

Trager, G. L.,   "An Outline of English Structure." In Austin,
and Smith,   W. M. (ed.). *Studies in Linguistics: Occasional*
H. L., Jr.   *Papers. #3, 1956.*

Trager, G. L.   "Paralanguage: A First Approximation." In
                  Austin, W. M. (ed.). *Studies in Linguistics.*
                  13:1–2 (spring) 1958.

Watzlawick,   *Pragmatics of Human Communication.* New
P., Beavin, J.,   York: Norton, 1967.
and Jackson,
D. D.

Wiener, N.   *Cybernetics; or, Control and Communication in*
                  the Animal and the Machine. New York: Wiley,
                  1948.

Wynne, L. C.,   "Pseudomutuality in the Family Relations of
Ryckoff,   Schizophrenia," *Psychiatry* 22:205, 1958.
I. M., Day, J.,
and Hirsch,
S. I.

Index

Whitaker, Carl, 23, 31, 69, 133, 137, 138, 141, 146, 151, 153–54
Wiener, N., 190
Winters, L. C., 42, 113

Youth and Sex: A Study of 1300 College Students (Bromley and Britten), 76